*Dedicated to
my dear wife Echo,
a faithful helper in the Lord*

Contents

Subject Guide
to Messages on Giving

Scripture Guide
to Messages on Giving

Foreword

Upon entering the pastorate, I resolved never to talk about money. Having previously served in several churches as an assistant, and having attended many others, I was sensitive to the complaint that "the church is always talking about money." And I knew there was some justification for that complaint. I resolved this would not be true of my ministry. I would not "say a word" about money.

That, however, did not relieve me of my responsibility as a pastor to perfect the saints (Ephesians 4:12), which includes seeing that they "abound in the grace of giving also" (II Corinthians 8:7).

Thus my plan was to present every Sunday a short message on giving. There would be no mention of money as such. The subject instead would be "giving." I realized, of course, that even this, done now and then, would bring the charge of "always talking about money." But if done every Sunday as a regular part of the service, it would be accepted and would not carry the pressure that occasionally mentioning giving, when there is a deficit or a project to be met, brings. The text of the message of the morning is repeated in the evening service without comment.

I acknowledge my indebtedness for this idea to Dr. Bartlett Hess, one of the pastors under whom I served as an assistant, whom I observed following a similar plan with good success.

The Scripture portions in these sermonettes are not always exact quotations from the King James Version, but are accurate renditions. Some may prefer to use other versions.

In addition to the brief messages in the pages that follow, letters from missionaries and stories and statistics from magazines and newspapers and other sources may be used.

I suggest that the minister who adopts this plan of mini-messages begin with a few messages from I Corinthians 16:2, establishing the concept of systematic, proportionate giving; then proceed through the series in II Corinthians 8 and 9, using one (or more) message on each verse, to give the basic New Testament teaching on giving. Then begin with Genesis and go through the whole series, occasionally interspersing other messages from I Corinthians 16:2 and additional ones from II Corinthians 8 and 9. The table of contents indicates some especially suitable ones for special days.

The term "systematic, proportionate giving" has been used more often than "tithes and offerings." Opinions vary on this; some reject the use of "tithes and offerings," asserting they belonged strictly to the Law. However, since tithes and offerings were offered as a means of systematic, proportionate giving before the Law—which was added because of transgression—was given, the phrases seem to say the same thing. The fact is, both Testaments teach systematic, proportionate giving, and it is the intent of these messages to cultivate such giving.

You may wish to have the binding cut off this book at a local print shop and put the pages in a file. Then, each week, one page could be taken to the pulpit.

As is apparent from the instances where several messages are based on the same text, there is no limit to the ideas that may be developed from any one text. These are offered as starters—as seed thoughts—for those who wish to see giving increase in their churches, and yet who do not wish to "say a word about money."

Raymond Bayne

GENESIS 14:20

And blessed be the most high God, which hath delivered thine enemies into thy hand. And he gave him tithes of all.

When God gave Abraham victory in a battle, Abraham gave tithes of all his gain to the priest of the most high God.

Here is an example of tithing before the Law. Involved was:

1. A recognition that all gain was of God.
2. A desire to show thanks in a material way.
3. A personal discipline, in the absence of a law, that would overcome any natural reluctance to give.
4. The application of a godly principle without any legal compulsion.

These same considerations will cause true Christians, also not under the Law, to practice systematic, proportionate giving.

PRAYER: Heavenly Father, aware that all we have is a gift from Thee, and desiring to show Thee our thanks with a proper proportion of it, we bring these tithes and offerings this morning and present them to Thee through Jesus Christ, our Lord. Amen.

GENESIS 28:22

And of all that thou shalt give me I will surely give the tenth to thee.

While God was dealing with Jacob in grace, Jacob said: "Of all that thou shalt give me, I will surely give the tenth unto thee (Genesis 28:22).

This was before the Law was given. It was the response of gratitude to the dealing of grace.

Even today, it is not in obedience to the Law, but in response to grace that we worship the Lord with our tithes and offerings (or, with our tenth).

PRAYER: Heavenly Father, we acknowledge that You have dealt with us in grace, doing for us the opposite of what we deserve because you cared for us. Give us a care for others that we may bring grace into their lives by our gifts, offered today through our Lord, Jesus Christ. Amen.

GENESIS 28:22

Of all that thou shalt give me I will surely give the tenth to thee.

When Jacob, like Abraham before him, said, "Of all that thou shalt give me I will surely give the tenth unto thee," he was acknowledging that the best way to accomplish anything is to have guidelines—a pattern—a standard. Little is accomplished by acting in a haphazard manner. Much is accomplished by being systematic.

God later taught this principle to all men by making tithing a part of the Law, so that we would not rob ourselves of His blessing by giving too little. He reaffirmed it in the New Testament by teaching systematic, proportionate giving.

Let us give systematically and proportionately as we worship the Lord.

PRAYER: Heavenly Father, we acknowledge our tendency to be careless in many areas of the Christian life, and especially in the area of giving. But in order to hear Your "well-done" at the end of life, we pray that You will teach us to be disciplined according to a set pattern in our giving. Here is our portion today, for Your use. In Jesus' name. Amen.

EXODUS 35:4-5

And Moses spake unto all the congregation of the children of Israel saying, This is the thing which the Lord commanded, saying, Take ye from among you an offering unto the Lord: whosoever is of a willing heart, let him bring it, an offering of the Lord. . . .

"This is the thing which the Lord commanded: Take from among you an offering unto the Lord; whosoever is of a willing heart, let him bring it."

"And they came, every one whose heart stirred him up, and every one whom his spirit made willing; and they brought the Lord's offering to the work" (35:21).

Again today, let those who have a willing heart bring an offering to the Lord for the work of the Lord.

PRAYER: Heavenly Father, help us to hearken to Your commands with a willing heart, and to bring an offering, not to the church but to You. Add Your blessing to that which we bring, that it may help people know the abundant life Christ gives, in whose name we pray. Amen.

LEVITICUS 25:20-21

And if ye shall say, what shall we eat the seventh year? behold, we shall not sow, nor gather in our increase: then I will command my blessing upon you in the sixth year, and it shall bring forth fruit for three years.

"If you shall say, What shall we eat the seventh year, if we do not sow, or gather in our increase? Then I will command my blessing upon you in the sixth year, and it shall bring forth fruit for three years."

God is saying here, if we will live by His laws we will not go hungry. Proportionate giving is both a law and a grace. If we will practice it, God will add His blessing to our efforts to provide for our families.

Let us trust and obey as we worship Him with our tithes and offerings.

PRAYER: Heavenly Father, when will we learn that there is no other way to enjoy security than to trust and obey? For the sake of the gospel in a world lost in sin, we obey Thee today in the matter of giving. Through our gifts may others learn to trust Jesus for eternal salvation. In Jesus' name. Amen.

LEVITICUS 27:30

And all the tithe of the land, whether of the seed of the land, or of the fruit of the tree, is the Lord's: it is holy unto the Lord.

"All the tithe . . . is the Lord's. It is holy unto the Lord."

You would not want to keep that which He has set apart to Himself, would you? And we can't say we cannot afford to give it to Him—to tithe.

God is concerned about our needs. He has promised to supply all our need. And, in the light of that fact, He has designated tithing—systematic, proportionate giving—as the basic method of giving for us all.

Then let us worship the Lord with His tithes and our offerings, and see Him supply our needs.

PRAYER: Heavenly Father, as we consider the ability and opportunity to earn what has been ours this week, may we have the faith and the desire to give Thee the tithe, that other people may be enriched with the gospel of our Lord, Jesus Christ. Amen.

And all the tithe of the land, whether of the seed of the land, or of the fruit of the tree, is the Lord's: it is holy unto the Lord.

"The tithe is the Lord's."

Louis XI, in a show of generosity, made a solemn deed in covenant, conveying the entire Province of Boulogne, France, to the Virgin Mary forever. "All the revenues thereof," however, he reserved for himself.

Some say, "Well, we're under grace and all we have belongs to God"—but they keep nearly all the *revenue* for themselves. I believe He would still prefer the tithe in cash.

Let us worship God with meaningful revenues today.

PRAYER: Heavenly Father, we bring Your tithes to You this morning. We would not pretend to honor You with gifts that are inadequate. All of our love is in our offering today. Bless its use as You have already blessed us, we pray in Jesus' name. Amen.

LEVITICUS 27:30-32

And all the tithe of the land, whether of the seed of the land, or of the fruit of the tree, is the Lord's: it is holy unto the Lord. And if a man will at all redeem ought of his tithes, he shall add thereto the fifth part thereof. And concerning the tithe of the herd, or of the flock, even of whatsoever passeth under the rod, the tenth shall be holy unto the Lord.

The Law says, "The tithe is the Lord's . . . the tenth shall be holy unto the Lord."

We are not under the Law, but the righteousness of the Law is to be fulfilled in us (Romans 8:4).

And the righteousness of the Law says that the only satisfactory way to recognize God's Lordship over all of our life is by systematically giving a definite percentage of our income.

And the redeemed person will be as anxious to do this under grace as God's people of the Old Testament were to do it under Law.

So let us fulfill the righteousness of the Law as we worship the Lord with His tithes and our offerings.

PRAYER: Heavenly Father, we would not sin that grace may abound; we would not withhold more than is right because we are not under the Law. We would give Thee what is right in Thy sight. In this spirit and in this measure we now present these offerings to Thee through our Lord, Jesus Christ. Amen.

NUMBERS 32:6
(Missionary Sunday)

And Moses said unto the children of Gad and to the children of Reuben, Shall your brethren go to war, and shall ye sit here?

The children of Reuben and Gad wanted to settle down, get ahead, and enrich themselves, while the rest of the Israelites went on to conquer Caanan.

Moses said, "Shall your brethren go to war and shall ye sit here?" He called for total mobilization.

We are in a spiritual battle today. The tide is against us. It is a time for total mobilization.

All of us can be actively engaged on the home front, calling and witnessing. We must also give to adequately maintain those on the distant fronts.

All citizens, in time of war, expect to be taxed in order to equip and sustain the citizens in the army.

As citizens of the heavenly kingdom, we are not taxed, but it is our privilege to give for this purpose as we worship the Lord with our systematic, proportionate gifts.

PRAYER: Heavenly Father, thank You for those who have gone to the front lines with the gospel. We would so give as to strengthen their hand and increase their victories. Help us to do our part well as we give through Jesus Christ, our Lord. Amen.

DEUTERONOMY 6:5

And thou shalt love the Lord thy God with all thine heart, and with all thy soul, and with all thy might.

MATTHEW 22:37

Jesus said unto him, Thou shalt love the Lord thy God with all thy heart, and with all thy soul, and with all thy mind.

God said it; Jesus reiterated it: "Thou shalt love the Lord thy God with all thine heart." Thus He binds us to Himself in the totality of our being. Everything comes under allegiance to Him, including what we do with our possessions.

When we recognize this we will also recognize that what counts in our giving is not our share in the budget of the church, but God's share of our income.

Systematic, proportionate giving is the only suitable way to do this. From this basis let us worship the Lord with our love offerings.

PRAYER: *Heavenly Father, we say we love Thee, and we do. But help us to love Thee with all our heart, and to show it by our gifts to Thee. There are so many needy hearts in the world, and we would help them in Thy name. To that end bless these gifts we bring this morning, through Jesus Christ, our Lord. Amen.*

DEUTERONOMY 8:11, 17-18

Beware that thou forget not the Lord thy God . . . and say in thine heart, My power and the might of mine hand hath gotten me this wealth. But thou shalt remember the Lord thy God, for it is he that giveth thee power to get wealth, that he may establish his covenant which he sware unto thy fathers, as it is this day.

Speaking of our possessions, whether many or few, Deuteronomy 8 says, "Beware . . . thou say not in thine heart, my power and the might of my hand hath gotten me this wealth. Thou shalt remember the Lord thy God; . . . it is he who gives thee power to get wealth."

Since this is so, it is right to thank God for what we have, to trust Him for what we need, and to give Him some in the same liberal fashion He has given us, that is, a proportionate gift.

With an awareness of the source of our resources, let us worship the Lord with our tithes and offerings.

PRAYER: *Heavenly Father, forgive our foolish pride and sense of proprietorship. We acknowledge by our giving today that all things come of Thee, and of Thine own have we given Thee. In Jesus' name. Amen.*

DEUTERONOMY 16:16-17
(Thanksgiving)

Three times in a year shall all thy males appear before the Lord thy God in the place which he shall choose; . . . and they shall not appear before the Lord empty. Every man shall give as he is able, according to the blessing of the Lord thy God which he hath given thee.

Concerning the Feast of Tabernacles, the Thanksgiving Day of the Bible, we read, "Thou shalt not appear before the Lord empty-handed. Every man shall give as he is able, according to the blessing of the Lord your God which He has given you."

Thanksgiving is not complete without an opportunity to do for others. Those who would truly give thanks seek opportunity to thankfully give.

Let us worship the Lord at this Thanksgiving time according to His blessing upon us.

PRAYER: Heavenly Father, You have daily loaded us with benefits. You have given with an open hand. You have met our every need, and more beside. Our offering today is an offering of thanks, of gratitude, to underscore what we have said with our lips. May it give others cause for thanksgiving as their lives are enriched by it, through Jesus Christ, our Lord. Amen.

DEUTERONOMY 26:10
(see whole chapter)

And now, behold, I have brought the firstfruits of the land, which thou, O Lord, hast given me. And thou shalt set it before the Lord thy God, and worship before the Lord thy God.

In Deuteronomy 26, God gave instructions for the offering. The person bringing the offering shall say: "Because the Lord has redeemed me . . . I have brought the firstfruits of the land [the first part of my income] which Thou, O Lord, hast given me . . . and Thou shalt set it before the Lord Thy God, and worship before the Lord Thy God."

Giving, you see, is an act of worship in gratitude for both redemption of the soul and the supplying of material need.

Let our offering be an act of grateful worship as we set before the Lord our first fruits.

PRAYER: Heavenly Father, how can we do less than give Thee our best since Thou art our Redeemer and Provider? With joy we bring our offering today, and worship Thee as we give it through Jesus Christ, our Lord. Amen.

And thou shalt set it before the Lord thy God, and worship before the Lord thy God.

Concerning the offering, Moses said, "Thou shalt set it before the Lord thy God."

Would it make any difference in our giving this morning if, instead of placing our envelopes in the offering plate, we placed them in the hands of the Lord Jesus Himself?

This, of course, is what we are actually doing; giving, not from our purse to the church, but from our heart to the Lord.

May this determine our giving as we worship the Lord with our systematic, proportionate giving.

PRAYER: Our Father, with all the respect, reverence, gratitude, and love of which Thou art deserving for all Thy goodness to us, we would set these offerings before Thee this morning. May they be acceptable because of the attitude of our hearts. Cause them to do good to the souls and lives of people, we pray in Jesus' name. Amen.

II SAMUEL 24:24

And the king said unto Araunah, Nay; but I will surely buy it of thee at a price: neither will I offer burnt offerings unto the Lord my God of that which doth cost me nothing. So David bought the threshingfloor and the oxen for fifty shekels of silver.

David said, "I will not offer . . . unto the Lord my God of that which cost me nothing."

Those who love God and are grateful for salvation do not give what they can spare; but by systematic, proportionate giving they regularly offer Him what He deserves, even if it hurts.

In this manner let us worship the Lord with our tithes and offerings this morning.

PRAYER: Heavenly Father, we are grateful for Your love shown toward us, in that while we were yet sinners, Christ died for us; and we do not want to give You what we don't feel. We want our heart to be in our gift, and so, this morning, we offer that portion of our income we think You are worthy of, through our Lord, Jesus Christ. Amen.

I CHRONICLES 29:3
(Building Fund)

Moreover, because I have set my affection to the house of my God, I have of mine own proper good, of gold and silver, which I have given to the house of my God, over and above all that I have prepared for the holy house.

David said, "Because I have set my affection upon the house of my God, I have of mine own proper goods, of gold and silver, . . . given to the house of my God."

When we have given ourselves to the Lord we will find it easy to give our substance. When we have set our affection on the house and work of God we will find it easy to give for their support. Giving begins in the heart.

May we give affectionately as we worship the Lord with our tithes and offerings.

PRAYER: Heavenly Father, we say we love Thee; we sing of our love for Thee; may we love Thee indeed, and may our love be shown in our giving as we bring Thee these gifts of our affection today, through Jesus Christ, our Lord. Amen.

I CHRONICLES 29:9
(Building Fund)

Then the people rejoiced, for that they offered willingly, because with perfect heart they offered willingly to the Lord: and David the king also rejoiced with great joy.

Concerning the giving of God's people for God's house and God's work, I Chronicles 29:9 says, "Then the people rejoiced . . . because with perfect heart they offered willingly to the Lord."

When we offer willingly, then it is fun to give; it is not painful; it is not with resentment; it is not with a feeling of being pressured; it is a joy.

God loves a cheerful giver because underneath is a perfect heart, offering willingly.

May He see that in us as we worship Him today with our systematic, proportionate gifts.

PRAYER: Heavenly Father, why shouldn't we offer willingly with a perfect heart when you have done so much for us, spiritually and materially? Search our hearts as we give today and see that we do love You and are glad to give in Jesus' name. Amen.

But who am I, and what is my people, that we should be able to offer so willingly after this sort? for all things come of thee, and of thine own have we given thee.

Concerning the offering, David said, "All things come of Thee, O Lord, and of Thine own have we given Thee."

It is good for us to keep this in mind. It is *not* that we have given God some of ours, and He should be thankful, but that we have given Him some of His and we should be thankful we have it to give. And we should be sure we are being good stewards, giving Him as much as we should, and doing with the rest what is pleasing to Him also.

In this spirit let us worship the Lord with our systematic, proportionate gifts.

PRAYER: Our Father, we thank Thee for everything we have, for every good gift which comes down from above. May we rightly understand what we are doing when we give; and may these gifts help other people in Jesus' name. Amen.

I CHRONICLES 29:14
(Building Fund)

But who am I, and what is my people, that we should be able to offer so willingly after this sort? for all things come of thee, and of thine own have we given thee.

When David had encouraged his people to give to the Lord's work and for the Lord's house, they gave liberally, and he said:

"Who am I, and what is my people, that we should be able to offer so willingly after this measure? For all things come of Thee, and of Thine own have we given Thee."

Their giving was not a duty and a burden, but a joy and a delight; not an obligation, but a privilege. They did not begrudge it; they enjoyed it.

So may we give for the work of the Lord here and abroad (and for our building program). (Comment about the Building Fund, if desired.)

PRAYER: Heavenly Father, in the spirit of David and his people, help us to understand that all we have, materially and spiritually, is from Thee, and to give Thee ourselves and our substance without restraint. May the zeal of Thy house urge us on. Sanctify these offerings we make to Thee today through Jesus Christ, our Lord. Amen.

But who am I, and what is my people, that we should be able to offer so willingly after this sort? for all things come of thee, and of thine own have we given thee.

"All things come of Thee, O Lord, and of Thine own have we given Thee."

As we approach the time for the offering, some ask themselves, "How much do I want to give of mine to the Lord?" Others ask, "How much of His may I rightly use for myself?"

Since we are "not our own, but are bought with a price—the blood of Jesus," surely the second question is more appropriate. Our giving is a dedication, a presentation, a yielding to the Lord of what is really His.

In so doing, we will:

never lack, for He is faithful to supply all our need;

never be unhappy, for it is more blessed to give than to receive; and

never be unfruitful, but will be abounding in the work of the Lord and laying up treasure in heaven.

Let us give Him a proper portion of that which He has given us.

PRAYER: We thank Thee, Father, for all Thy help this week, and the provision of all our need. Week after week, and year after year our needs are supplied and we thank Thee, with these words, and with these offerings, that we make to Thee now. Through them bless other families, we pray in Jesus' name. Amen.

I CHRONICLES 29:17
(Building Fund)

I know also, my God, that thou triest the heart, and hast pleasure in uprightness. As for me, in the uprightness of mine heart I have willingly offered all these things, and now have I seen with joy thy people, which are present here, to offer willingly unto thee.

Concerning his offering for the Lord's house and work, David said, I Chronicles 29:17, "In the uprightness of my heart I have willingly offered all these things."

It is good to drop one's offering in the plate with a clear conscience, knowing that it is not done grudgingly or out of a sense of obligation, but willingly. It makes it so much more enjoyable to give and God is more delighted with it.

May we have that consciousness of willing giving as we worship the Lord today with our tithes and offerings.

PRAYER: Heavenly Father, we would search our hearts, as we know You do, as we present our offerings today, to be sure there is not the slightest trace of resentment or stinginess about giving to One who spared not His own Son but delivered Him up for us all, and with Him has freely given us all things. Make these gifts a blessing to other people, we pray in Jesus' name. Amen.

Blessed is he that considereth the poor: the Lord will deliver him in time of trouble. The Lord will preserve him, and keep him alive; and he shall be blessed upon the earth: and thou wilt not deliver him unto the will of his enemies. The Lord will strengthen him upon the bed of languishing: thou wilt make all his bed in his sickness.

"Blessed is he that considereth the poor:
The Lord will deliver him in time of trouble;
The Lord will preserve him and keep him alive;
[The Lord will] bless him upon the earth;
[The Lord] will not deliver him unto the will of his enemies;
The Lord will strengthen him;
[The Lord] will make his bed in sickness."

God delights to see an unselfish, generous heart, and over and over again promises to return blessings of all kinds on those who give in consideration of the needs of others. No one can honestly say, "I cannot afford to give."

Let us consider a world in need as we worship the Lord with our systematic, proportionate giving.

PRAYER: Heavenly Father, truly we ought to give, just because we love our neighbor as ourselves. But we are encouraged in our giving by Your many promises. We pray especially today for those who have never heard the gospel, that they may be blessed by our gifts today, offered through the merit of One who gave Himself for us. Amen.

For every beast of the forest is mine, and the cattle upon a thousand hills. . . .
If I were hungry, I would not tell thee: for the world is mine, and the fullness
thereof.

"Every beast of the forest is mine, and the cattle upon a thousand
hills. . . . If I were hungry, I would not tell thee; for the world is mine,
and the fullness thereof."

God does not need our help or our gifts. But He graciously invites us
to help and give, and deigns to use what we give Him, and even makes
His work dependent on what we give Him.

Then how much shall we give? Does it make any difference? Yes; in
two ways: The measure in which we give indicates the measure of our
love for Him and our interest in His work; and it determines how
much can be accomplished for Him.

Let us consider what would be a worthy proportion to give as we
worship the Lord with our tithes and offerings.

PRAYER: *Heavenly Father, let us not be content to declare our love for
Thee with words only. Here are our gifts, a part of our substance, a part of
ourselves; and a proportion, we trust, sufficient to say, "We love Thee most
of all." In our Savior's merit receive them. Amen.*

PSALM 68:19
(Thanksgiving)

Blessed be the Lord, who daily loadeth us with benefits, even the God of our
salvation.

"Blessed be the Lord, who daily loadeth us with benefits, even the
God of our salvation."

In appreciation of these spiritual and material benefits, and out of
the abundance of them, feeling that we can afford to because He has so
well taken care of us, we bring our gifts from week to week, that others
may know these benefits.

In this way let us worship the God of our salvation.

PRAYER: *Heavenly Father, though words fail us to express our gratitude
and adoration, we would express it in some measure by our offerings,
perhaps entailing a sacrifice, but given freely and in love, through Jesus
Christ, our Lord. Amen.*

PSALM 95:2
(Thanksgiving)

Let us come before his presence with thanksgiving, and make a joyful noise unto him with psalms.

"Let us come before his presence with thanksgiving."

Thanksgiving may be rightly understood as "giving thanks," or "giving in thanks" (or "thankfully giving"); and we ought to do both.

Most families eat well all year, but at Thanksgiving they spend extra and eat more. And most Christian families give all year, but at Thanksgiving they give extra, to give tangible expression to their thanksgiving.

With thankful hearts, let us worship the Lord with the "sacrifices of thanksgiving" (Psalm 107:22).

PRAYER: Heavenly Father, with thankful hearts we come to worship. With thankful hearts we sing Thy praise. And with thankful hearts we bring our offerings, thankful that we can give to Thee and that Thou wilt use it that others may have cause for thanksgiving. In Jesus' name. Amen.

PSALM 112:9

He hath dispersed, he hath given to the poor; his righteousness endureth for ever; his horn shall be exalted with honour.

Psalm 112:9 describes a child of God who gives: "He hath distributed freely; he hath given to the poor; his righteousness endureth for ever; he is highly esteemed."

God observes the practical righteousness of our giving to bless other lives, and rewards it. Thus, we don't really lose; we gain. Once again, then, we see it is more blessed to give than to receive.

Let us exercise this practical righteousness as we worship the Lord with our distribution.

PRAYER: Heavenly Father, help us as we give today to be aware that you see what we give and that by it You measure our practical righteousness, and value it accordingly. Put a generous spirit in us. May we not deprive our needy neighbor, or You, or ourselves of the good that comes from giving. Through the merit of Jesus we offer these gifts. Amen.

PSALM 116:12
(Taxes)

What shall I render unto the Lord for all his benefits toward me?

April 15th is that happy day that comes once a year when we pay for the benefits we receive as citizens of this wonderful country.

Psalm 116:12 asks, "What shall I render unto the Lord for all his benefits toward me?"

May I suggest we compare our total tax with our total giving to the Lord last year for the great benefits we have received from Him, and see if we have done well.

Let us continue to render unto the Lord for His continuing benefits as we worship Him now with our tithes and offerings.

PRAYER: Heavenly Father, we agree with the psalmist that You daily load us with benefits, including the benefit of employment and income so we have the occasion and means to say thanks. And just as our government requires our tax of us whether we think we can afford it or not, may we require it of ourselves to give unto You through our Lord, Jesus Christ, Amen.

PROVERBS 3:9

Honour the Lord with thy substance, and with the firstfruits of all thine increase.

"Honour the Lord with thy substance, and with the first fruits of all thine increase."

In our giving, and in the handling of all our funds, what we give to God should be the first fruits.

When we give out of what is left after we pay our bills and spend on ourselves, we indicate the place we give God and how important we think He is in our everyday life.

Since God is worthy of first place, and is not only necessary, but important to our lives, we should give to Him first and take care of our own needs afterward. And when we do, He promises our own needs will be abundantly met.

May our worship of the Lord with our substance be a testimony this morning that we are giving Him first place in our lives.

PRAYER: Heavenly Father, our Creator and Redeemer, and the One who has provided our every need, Thou art worthy of receiving the first portion of our income, and we bring it this morning and offer it to Thee in loving gratitude through Jesus Christ, our Lord. Amen.

PROVERBS 3:9

Honour the Lord with thy substance, and with the firstfruits of all thine increase.

"Honor the Lord with thy substance, and with the firstfruits of all thine increase."

For those who look on the offering as a nuisance, or a necessary evil, or who resent it, or whose image of the church is that it is always asking for money, Proverbs 3:9 is a reminder that our giving is more than paying for the expenses of the church and the spread of the gospel. It is a way of honoring the Lord. It is an act of worship. It is to be done with a glad and willing heart.

Let God be honored today as we worship the Lord with our first fruits.

PRAYER: Heavenly Father, we confess we have not always had a good attitude toward giving and the needs brought to our attention. Help us to get our eyes off ourselves and learn the joy of honoring Thee in our giving. Receive our offerings today through Jesus Christ. Amen.

PROVERBS 3:9

Honour the Lord with thy substance, and with the firstfruits of all thine increase.

Throughout the heathen world, people give their most precious possessions to their gods, often resulting in poverty for themselves. This they do out of fear, for their own salvation. Christians give out of love, because they have salvation. Surely this love will prompt us to give liberally out of our whole income, rather than out of what is left after we have spent on ourselves.

Let us "honor the Lord with our substance, and with the firstfruits of all our increase," as we worship Him with gifts of love.

PRAYER: Heavenly Father, thank You for the free gift of salvation. We bring our gifts of love, a worthy part of our whole income, and not a part of a part. Use these offerings to bring salvation to others, we pray in Jesus' name. Amen.

PROVERBS 3:9
(Taxes)

Honour the Lord with thy substance, and with the firstfruits of all thine increase.

"Honor the Lord with thy substance, and with the firstfruits of all thine increase."

We are all familiar with the terms "withholding tax" and "take-home pay." Most of us would find it very difficult to pay our taxes if we waited until it was convenient. And so our government has arranged to take our tax out before giving us our paycheck, knowing our weakness.

This is God's plan too, not only because He knows our weakness, but to signify the honor that belongs to Him. "On the first day of the week, let every one of you lay by him in store, as God hath prospered him" (I Corinthians 16:2).

With Uncle Sam it is a tax; with God it is an offering. Will we do less for love than for law? Let us worship the Lord out of this week's increase.

PRAYER: Heavenly Father, thank You for all the benefits we receive from Your hand. May our acknowledgement of them prompt us to give so that others may share in them too. Bless these offerings we bring You now in the building up of Your kingdom, through Jesus Christ, our Lord. Amen.

PROVERBS 3:9-10

Honour the Lord with thy substance, and with the firstfruits of all thine increase: so shall thy barns be filled with plenty, and thy presses shall burst out with new wine.

"Honor the Lord with thy substance, and with the firstfruits of all thine increase; so shall thy barns be filled with plenty."

The key to prosperity and having all our needs met is to give God His portion first.

Let us worship the Lord with His tithes and our offerings.

PRAYER: Heavenly Father, we would learn your ways from a continual study of Your Word, and then would be doers of the Word and not hearers only. May we learn well this lesson concerning our personal finances and live by it from week to week, that You may be honored and our pantries well stocked. For Jesus' sake. Amen.

PROVERBS 3:9-10

Honour the Lord with thy substance, and with the firstfruits of all thine increase: so shall thy barns be filled with plenty, and thy presses shall burst out with new wine.

"Honor the Lord with thy substance, and with the first fruits of all thine increase; so shall thy barns be filled with plenty."

Faith is man's active response to God's revelation in His Word.

In His Word God reveals that He will supply the daily needs of those who give to supply the needs of others. Here is a good place to venture out on the life of faith, not with some great and mighty deed, but with systematic, proportionate giving as on the first day of each week you give a definite percentage of your income to the Lord. Faith will not say, "I can't afford it"; but rather, "I believe God and that it shall be even as it was told me."

In faith, then, let us worship the Lord with the first part of our income.

PRAYER: Heavenly Father, thank You for the things You have revealed. Help us not to be selective in the things we believe and respond to. And in this matter that touches us daily and weekly, may our faith be strong. As we present these evidences of our faith and concern, we trust You to supply our own need. In Jesus' name. Amen.

Honour the Lord with thy substance, and with the firstfruits of all thine increase: so shall thy barns be filled with plenty, and thy presses shall burst out with new wine.

R. B. Oliver tells of old Zagni, who loved to help others in need, and to earn money for her Lord. On one occasion she injured her foot, and it was nine months before she could walk or work again.

Eager to make up for lost time, she promised the missionary that she would begin to make and sell bean cakes once more. Instead of giving the Lord a tithe, she would give Him one-third of the first three shillings she earned.

The missionary was surprised when she soon returned with one shilling. "You surely haven't earned three shillings already!" she said with surprise. Old Zagni was shocked. "Do you think I would give my Lord the last of the three?" she asked. "This is the first; the other two will be for me."

When all Christians feel this way, the Lord's work will go forward. "Honor the Lord with thy substance, and with the firstfruits of all thine increase; so shall thy barns be filled with plenty" (Proverbs 3:9-10).

Let us honor the Lord today with the first fruits of what we have earned this week.

PRAYER: Heavenly Father, thank You for folks like Zagni. Give us a heart like hers. May our love for You overwhelm all our selfishness and make us zealous in giving. We offer our first fruits this morning through Jesus Christ, our Lord. Amen.

PROVERBS 3:28

Say not unto thy neighbour, Go, and come again, and tomorrow I will give; when thou hast it by thee.

"Say not unto thy neighbor, Go and come again, and tomorrow I will give; when thou hast it by thee."

The time to give is when need and opportunity present themselves. Procrastination is a sure way to kill a generous impulse, and lose an opportunity to be a blessing.

God's provision of our needs is the opportunity; the world's condition is the need. So let us worship the Lord *now* with our gifts.

PRAYER: Heavenly Father, help us to see that as long as we have more than others, there is both need and opportunity to give, and so may we give. Here are our gifts today, offered in the merit of Jesus, our Lord. Amen.

PROVERBS 4:23

Keep thy heart with all diligence; for out of it are the issues of life.

"Out of [the heart] are the issues of life."

Giving, like serving, is more important for its spiritual significance than its financial significance; more important for its indication of the place we have given the Lord in our lives than for its help in paying the bills incurred in the Lord's work.

A heart that is unselfish, trusting, dedicated, and having a sense of stewardship is of more concern to God than the financial needs of His work.

It is well to examine our hearts as we worship the Lord with our systematic, proportionate giving.

PRAYER: Heavenly Father, we profess to love Thee and trust Thee. May it be apparent in what we give to Thee this day through Jesus Christ, our Lord. Amen.

There is he that scattereth, and yet increaseth; and there is that withholdeth more than is meet, but it tendeth to poverty.

POSSESSIONS

There was only a little oil in the cruse,
  A handful of meal in the bin;
But the prophet asked the widow to share
  The little she had with him.
And all through the famine, long and dread,
  The widow, her son, and the prophet had bread.

There was only a lad with five barley cakes
  And a couple of fishes small,
But the Master's blessing went with the gift
  And fed the multitude, all.
And down through the ages the story will live,
  Of the little boy who was willing to give.

"But, Lord, my possessions are poor and mean.
  You know I need them all.
If I had wealth, I would gladly hear
  And answer the needy's call."
So I grasp my little with greedy hands—
But it slips through my fingers like sift-
  ing sands.

Myra A. Hart

"There is he that scattereth, and yet increaseth. There is he that withholdeth more than is suitable, but it tendeth to poverty."

Moved by the need of others, let us worship the Lord by scattering our possessions.

PRAYER: *Heavenly Father, we think of all the good that has been done for others by giving (without any harm to the givers), and we would join the givers that others may have the Bread of life. Multiply the gifts we offer through Jesus Christ, our Lord. Amen.*

There is that maketh himself rich, yet hath nothing; there is that maketh himself poor, yet hath great riches.

"There is that maketh himself rich, yet hath nothing; there is that maketh himself poor, yet hath great riches."

According to God's Word, true riches come not from keeping—for self, but by giving—for others.

Let us accumulate true riches as we worship the Lord with our tithes and offerings.

PRAYER: *Heavenly Father, help us to be aware of those who have less than we, materially or spiritually, and to reduce our own substance that they might increase theirs, after the pattern of our Lord Jesus, "who, though he was rich, yet for our sakes became poor, that we through his poverty might be rich." Amen.*

PROVERBS 19:17

He that hath pity upon the poor lendeth unto the Lord; and that which he hath given will he pay him again.

"He that hath pity on the poor lendeth unto the Lord; and that which he hath given will the Lord pay him again."

What a collateral! What a co-signer!

When you lend money to people, you are not always sure you will get it back. For this reason a collateral or a co-signer is often required. But even they may fail in their obligation. But here is a collateral that is posted and signed by God Himself! What an inspiration to give! And what a fine sense of justice God has.

With consideration of the poor, and the assurance that our own needs will be supplied, let us worship the Lord with our systematic, proportionate giving.

PRAYER: *Heavenly Father, the more we read of Your ways, the more we are amazed. How often You condescend to strengthen our weak faith and allay our fears for our own security. With grateful hearts, and a special concern for those who are spiritually poor, we give through our Lord, Jesus Christ. Amen.*

He that hath pity upon the poor lendeth unto the Lord; and that which he hath given will he pay him again.

"He that hath pity upon the poor lendeth unto the Lord [when you lend something, you get it back; when you give to help others, you are lending to the Lord]; and that which you give will the Lord pay you again."

We do not give to get; we do not give with ulterior motives; but God will not be in debt to any man. And many Scripture passages assure us that giving never makes any one poorer. In fact, when you lend, you get it back with interest; and that is the way God deals with us.

It is such a God as this we worship with our systematic, proportionate giving.

PRAYER: Heavenly Father, Your ways are marvelous in our eyes. Give us a pity for the poor that will constrain us to help them, and help us to trust You for our needs. In Jesus' name. Amen.

PROVERBS 28:27

He that giveth unto the poor shall not lack: but he that hideth his eyes shall have many a curse.

"He that giveth unto the poor shall not lack: but he that hideth his eyes shall have many a curse."

We do not give to keep the church running; we give to meet the needs of the poor—those poor spiritually or materially.

And God's blessing is on those who consider the needs of others. Liberality will not make anyone poor; nor will it be unrewarded in this life or the next.

Let us consider the needs of others as we worship the Lord with our gifts.

PRAYER: Heavenly Father, help us to have the mind of Christ, a mind attuned to the needs of others; to look not on our own needs and wants, but on the deeper needs of others, and to give that their needs may be met. To this end bless these offerings we bring today through our Lord, Jesus Christ. Amen.

He that giveth unto the poor shall not lack: but he that hideth his eyes shall have many a curse.

Bills piling up faster than you can keep up? See Malachi 3:10-11. To those who brought their tithes to the Lord, He said, "I will rebuke the devourer for your sakes."

If you are tempted to say, "If God prospers me I will give," think again. God's plan for having enough to give is for us to prime our own pump. Proverbs 28:27 promises that "he that gives . . . shall not lack"; and Luke 6:38 says, "Give, and it shall be given unto you."

So it's not "I will be able to give if God will give to me," but "If I will give to Him He will supply my need." Do you dare believe this?

Let us give in faith as we worship the Lord with our tithes and offerings.

PRAYER: Heavenly Father, forgive us for so often getting things backward to our own disadvantage. Forgive us for our lack of faith in Your faithfulness to Your promises and Your ways. This morning we give in faith, and thank You that You will supply our needs as your children. In Jesus' name. Amen.

HAGGAI 1:6

Ye have sown much, and bring in little; ye eat, but ye have not enough; ye drink, but ye are not filled with drink; ye clothe you, but there is none warm; and he that earneth wages earneth wages to put it into a bag with holes.

As you may have read, the Penn-Central Railroad auctioned off some of its museum pieces to help pay its debts. Old tickets which wouldn't be accepted anywhere brought $1.00. Old menus which wouldn't feed you anything brought $60.00. Old wheels which wouldn't take you anywhere brought $2,000.00.

Not so with those who give to the Lord. What they give is accepted by God Himself to feed others the Bread of life and take those who believe to heaven. How much better an investment this is! Haggai 1:6 speaks of "putting money into a bag with holes." That is what the world is doing.

But we are investing our money in eternal things when we worship the Lord with our systematic, proportionate giving.

PRAYER: Heavenly Father, help us keep our sense of values straight. While we enjoy some of the many things you have given us to enjoy, help us to remember those who have little to enjoy, and little heart to enjoy it because they do not have the Savior, in whose name and for whose sake we bring these offerings this morning. Amen.

MALACHI 3:8

Will a man rob God? Yet ye have robbed me. But ye say, Wherein have we robbed thee? In tithes and offerings.

"Will a man rob God? Yet ye have robbed me. But ye say, how have we robbed thee? In tithes and offerings." The tithe is the Lord's. To withhold it is to rob Him.

Men would not believe they would kill God—until Jesus came and they crucified Him. And men will not believe they would rob God till they get their paycheck and see so many things they want for themselves they are unwilling to give God that which belongs to Him.

Let us not rob God, but worship Him with His tithes and our offerings.

PRAYER: Heavenly Father, because we are not under the Law, but under grace, may the sin of using all we have for ourselves not have dominion over us. May the righteousness of the law of systematic, proportionate giving be fulfilled in us as we bring our offerings today and offer them through the merit of our Redeemer, and in response to His great gift. Amen.

MALACHI 3:8

Will a man rob God? Yet ye have robbed me. But ye say, Wherein have we robbed thee? In tithes and offerings.

In that familiar portion of Malachi where God accuses His people of robbing Him, He says it is by withholding tithes and offerings; not just tithes, but offerings, too. If we have learned the grace of tithing, let us not be smugly content the rest of our lives, but go on to learn the grace of offerings.

Indeed, let us worship the Lord now with our tithes and offerings.

PRAYER: Heavenly Father, not the least, but the best we would give Thee; not what is required only, but what our hearts prompt us to do in gratitude; not a minimum, but all that our means make possible we would give to Thee through our Lord, Jesus Christ. Amen.

MALACHI 3:8

Will a man rob God? Yet ye have robbed me. But ye say, Wherein have we robbed thee? In tithes and offerings.

TIPPING AND TITHING

Now it came to pass on a Day at Noon that the Editor was a Guest of a certain rich man. And the Lunch was enjoyed at a popular Restaurant. And the Waiters were very efficient. And the Food was good.

Now when the End of the Meal was at Hand, the Waiters brought unto the Host the Check. And the Host examined it, frowned a bit, but made no comment.

But as we arose to depart, I observed that he laid some Coins under the Edge of his Plate. Howbeit, I know not what Denomination the Coins were.

But the Waiter who stood near by smiled happily which, being interpreted, means that the Tip was satisfactory.

Now with such Customs we are all familiar. And this Parable entereth not into the Merits or Demerits of Tipping.

But as I meditated on the Coins that become Tips throughout our Nation, I began to think of Tips and Tithes. For the Proverbial Tip should be at least a Tithe, lest the Waiter or Waitress turn against you.

And as I continued to think on these things, it came unto me that few People who go to Church treat their God as well as they honor their Waiter. For they give unto the Waiter a Tithe, but unto God they give whatsoever they think will get them by.

Verily, doth Man fear the Waiter more than he feareth God? And doth he love God less than he loveth the Waiter?

Truly, truly, a Man and his Money are past Understanding!

(reprinted from *Honeywell Sensor News*, Honeywell, Inc. Used by permission.)

Malachi anticipated this story when he asked, "Will a man rob God . . . in tithes and offerings?"

Let our response be an emphatic No as we please and honor and worship Him with our proportionate gifts.

PRAYER: Heavenly Father, we would treat Thee best of all, for Thou art worthy of our all. Receive and use these offerings, we pray, through Jesus Christ, our Lord. Amen.

MALACHI 3:8
(Year's End)

Will a man rob God? Yet ye have robbed me. But ye say, Wherein have we robbed thee? In tithes and offerings.

Malachi asked, "Will a man rob God?" Another translation has it: "Will a man defraud God?"—that is, "cover up what he is doing?"

In answer Malachi said, "Bring all the tithe to the Lord." He didn't say they were not giving; but they were not giving proportionately. So what they were doing was covering up what they were not doing.

Sometimes we think we are giving enough when we give a large amount. But that large gift may cover up the fact that we are not giving proportionately, which is God's plan for our giving.

Surely, none of us wants to defraud God. We can best avoid this by systematic, proportionate giving, and we recommend this for the coming year.

Let us do this now as we worship the Lord with a proportionate gift.

PRAYER: Heavenly Father, how could we think of withholding from You when You withheld not Your own Son, but delivered Him up for us all. We would bring today, not only our offerings, but our commitment to systematic, proportionate giving. May these offerings bring the words of eternal life to some who have never heard of Him in whose name we offer them. Amen.

MALACHI 3:8-9

Will a man rob God? Yet ye have robbed me. But ye say, Wherein have we robbed thee? In tithes and offerings. Ye are cursed with a curse: for ye have robbed me, even this whole nation.

In Malachi 3:8 God said to His people, "Will a man rob God?"

They were upset and said, "How can we do that?"—reach into heaven and take something? No. Steal from the church? No.

"In tithes and offerings" God said—in keeping back for self a part that belongs to God.

And when we rob God we rob ourselves. Malachi 3:9 adds, "Ye are cursed with a curse; for ye have robbed me."

Is it possible we would never think of robbing people, but regularly rob God? Let's not rob Him this morning. Let's worship the Lord with His tithes and our offerings.

PRAYER: Heavenly Father, You give to us before we give and after we give. Then forbid that we should keep back part of what we should give to You. These are our systematic, proportionate gifts. Use them for Your own purposes. Amen.

MALACHI 3:10
(Year's End)

Bring ye all the tithes into the storehouse, that there may be meat in mine house, and prove me now herewith, saith the Lord of hosts, if I will not open you the windows of heaven, and pour you out a blessing, that there shall not be room enough to receive it.

During this past year many of us have practiced systematic, proportionate giving—tithing—giving 10 percent or more of our income to the Lord. Is there anyone here who has done this who can stand and testify that God has not supplied your need? (Pause.)

If you are a tither you can be as sure God will supply your need as you can be sure of salvation; both are promised in God's Word.

Malachi 3:10: "Bring all the tithes into the storehouse . . . and prove me now herewith, saith the Lord of hosts, if I will not open for you the windows of heaven, and pour out for you a blessing, that there shall not be room enough to receive it."

First Corinthians 16:2: "On the first day of the week let every one of you lay by him in store, as God hath prospered him."

We testify at this year's end to God's faithfulness in fulfilling these promises, and recommend this method of stewardship for the coming year.

Those who use it are always ready to worship the Lord with their tithes and offerings.

PRAYER: Heavenly Father, how gracious are Your ways. You provide our need, and then promise to give more if we give You back our tithes and offerings. And we have seen You faithfully keep these promises. May we have faith to be faithful in our stewardship, and give as we ought through Jesus Christ, our Lord. Amen.

MALACHI 3:10
(Tithing Month)

Bring ye all the tithes into the storehouse, that there may be meat in mine house, and prove me now herewith, saith the Lord of hosts, if I will not open you the windows of heaven, and pour you out a blessing, that there shall not be room enough to receive it.

"Bring all the tithes into the storehouse, that there may be food in mine house, and prove me now herewith, saith the Lord of hosts, if I will not open for you the windows of heaven, and pour out for you a blessing, that there shall not be room enough to receive it."

Don't you marvel at God's ways? First He asks us to tithe—whatever our income, to give 10 percent to Him; then He promises to supply our need if we do. Then He invites us to do it on a trial basis and see. Then He promises to do more than make the nine tenths go as far as the ten tenths; He promises to give back more than we give.

You can't beat a proposition like that, can you? You can't outgive a God like that.

This is "Prove Me Month." For your own discovery we are inviting those who have not had the faith or the courage or the grace to try tithing, to try God and see how He works.

Those who have tried Him are now prepared to worship the Lord with their systematic, proportionate gifts.

PRAYER: Heavenly Father, our Creator, Redeemer, and Provider, we worship Thee this morning, not only with our words, but with our substance, so that others may worship Thee too, through the personal knowledge of Christ gained by means of our gifts. Amen.

MALACHI 3:10
(Tithing Month)

Bring ye all the tithes into the storehouse, that there may be meat in mine house, and prove me now herewith, saith the Lord of hosts, if I will not open you the windows of heaven, and pour you out a blessing, that there shall not be room enough to receive it.

"Bring all the tithes into the storehouse, that there may be food in my house, and prove me now herewith, saith the Lord of hosts, if I will not open for you the windows of heaven, and pour out for you a blessing, that there shall not be room enough to receive it."

Isn't it gracious of God to actually invite us to prove Him; the creatures to prove the Creator, to see if we can really afford to tithe, to see if He will provide our material needs if we are faithful in giving 10 percent of our income to Him?

We are suggesting that this month be "Prove Me Month," especially for those who haven't had the courage to try tithing. We predict once you start, you will never quit.

Let's embark on such an experiment this morning as we worship the Lord with our tithes and offerings.

PRAYER: Heavenly Father, thank You for Your patience with us, and for inviting us to give on a trial basis. Those of us who have tried it, thank You that You kept Your promises, and our needs have been met. Again today we present our offerings through our Lord, Jesus Christ. Amen.

MALACHI 3:10
(Tithing Month)

Bring ye all the tithes into the storehouse, that there may be meat in mine house, and prove me now herewith, saith the Lord of hosts, if I will not open you the windows of heaven, and pour you out a blessing, that there shall not be room enough to receive it.

"Bring ye all the tithes into the storehouse, that there may be food in my house, and prove me now herewith, saith the Lord of hosts, if I will not open for you the windows of heaven, and pour out for you a blessing, that there shall not be room enough to receive it."

Can you, or can you not, afford to give on the basis of God's promise to supply your need if you will give to Him? God invites you to prove Him and see. When do you do that? Unless it is scheduled, you might deprive yourself of His blessing for a long time.

We are suggesting this month be "Prove Me Month"; an opportunity for some to see how God can make 90 percent go as far as 100 percent.

Trusting His promises, let us all worship the Lord this morning as we bring the tithes to Him.

PRAYER: Heavenly Father, we marvel again that the Creator would invite the creature to prove Him; that our Redeemer would invite the redeemed to test His promises. And we testify that Your promises are dependable. In faith, which works by love, we bring our offerings today through Jesus Christ, our Lord. Amen.

MALACHI 3:10
(Tithing Month)

Bring ye all the tithes into the storehouse, that there may be meat in mine house, and prove me now herewith, saith the Lord of hosts, if I will not open you the windows of heaven, and pour you out a blessing, that there shall not be room enough to receive it.

"Bring ye all the tithes into the storehouse, that there may be food in my house, and prove me now herewith, saith the Lord of hosts, if I will not open for you the windows of heaven, and pour out for you a blessing that there shall not be room enough to receive it."

Those who invest money know that their return is based on the amount of their investment; the more they invest the more they get back.

Just so in this matter of tithing. God's invitation to prove Him is based on bringing "all" the tithe to Him. Bring some and He will provide for you. Bring it all and He will "pour" you out a blessing that will overflow.

This is "Prove Me Month"—to test God and see if He really does in this twentieth century what He promised long ago to do. If you haven't dared to tithe, dare to test God this month.

Those who dare are now ready to worship the Lord with their tithes and offerings.

PRAYER: Heavenly Father, teach us Your ways; teach us to trust You and obey You. Thank You that You are willing to be tested out, and that You are trustworthy. On the basis of Your promise, we bring our offering this morning, and offer it through Jesus Christ, our Lord. Amen.

MALACHI 3:10
(Tithing Month)

Bring ye all the tithes into the storehouse, that there may be meat in mine house, and prove me now herewith, saith the Lord of hosts, if I will not open you the windows of heaven, and pour you out a blessing, that there shall not be room enough to receive it.

"Bring ye all the tithes into the storehouse, that there may be food in mine house, and test me now herewith, saith the Lord of hosts, if I will not open for you the windows of heaven, and pour out for you a blessing, that there shall not be room enough to receive it."

We are suggesting this month as "Prove Me Month." Someone told me recently, "Since we have been tithing, God has never failed to supply our need."

That's what He promised, and He invites everyone of us to prove Him, to see if He will make the nine tenths go as far as ten tenths.

If you haven't proved Him yet, try it this month; you just might let yourself in on a blessing.

Let's worship the Lord now with our tithes and offerings.

PRAYER: Heavenly Father, thank You for Your faithful provision of our need every day; already You have proved Yourself. May we prove ourselves—our trust, our gratitude, our generous spirit, our stewardship as we give to You today, and every day, through Jesus Christ, our Lord. Amen.

MALACHI 3:10
(Tax Time)

Bring ye all the tithes into the storehouse, that there may be meat in mine house, and prove me now herewith, saith the Lord of hosts, if I will not open you the windows of heaven, and pour you out a blessing, that there shall not be room enough to receive it.

"Bring ye all the tithes . . . saith the Lord."

It is a good testimony that several of our people have been called in by the Bureau of Internal Revenue to explain their large deduction for giving to the church. In many cases, the simple explanation that they are tithers is all that is required. In others, written statements from the church indicating what they have put in their envelope week by week has substantiated their claim.

It is true that the per capita giving of tithers is higher than most, and much higher than the average. This kind of giving by all will enable more to be done for God, here and abroad.

Let us worship the Lord with our tithes and offerings.

PRAYER: Heavenly Father, we are grateful that our government recognizes tithing as a divinely established principle, and approves of its practice for the welfare of our country. May we be faithful in giving our Christian testimony to them by our systematic, proportionate giving, through Jesus Christ, our Lord. Amen.

Bring ye all the tithes into the storehouse, that there may be meat in mine house, and prove me now herewith, saith the Lord of hosts, if I will not open you the windows of heaven, and pour you out a blessing, that there shall not be room enough to receive it.

There are many aspects of the Christian life, each of which reveals something about a person and his relationship to the Lord. Giving is one of these aspects.

Some families with a modest income and two or three children faithfully give a tithe—10 percent—of their income to the Lord and His work. Others in the same circumstances, or better, give 1 or 2 percent.

Obviously it is not what we can afford to give, but what we want to give that determines our offering; not our circumstances, but our heart that makes the difference.

As a Christian recognizes his stewardship, for which he is responsible before God, and prays about his giving, he will find that systematic, proportionate giving is the only way to give what he should, and that is the key to personal prosperity.

Malachi 3:10 says, "Bring all the tithes into the storehouse, that there may be food in mine house, and prove me now herewith, saith the Lord of hosts, if I will not open for you the windows of heaven, and pour out for you a blessing, that there shall not be room enough to receive it."

PRAYER: Heavenly Father, with loving hearts and grateful spirits we would bring our systematic, proportionate giving to Thee. Bless it in the ministry of Thy Word as we offer it through Jesus Christ, our Lord. Amen.

Bring ye all the tithes into the storehouse, that there may be meat in mine house, and prove me now herewith, saith the Lord of hosts, if I will not open you the windows of heaven, and pour you out a blessing, that there shall not be room enough to receive it.

ON TITHING

I wonder why the Lord did ask
For tithes from you and me;
When all the treasures of the earth
Are His—eternally?

And why should He depend on us
To fill His house with meat;
When we have so very little
And His storehouse is replete?

But He said to bring our little,
And He would add His much;
Then all the heavenly windows
Would be opened at His touch.

And blessings running over—
Even more than has been told—
Will be ours; but there's no promise
If His portion we withhold!

Are we afraid to prove Him?
Is our faith and love so small
That we tightly grasp our little
When He freely gave His all?

Author Unknown

Let us worship the Lord as we bring our tithes and offerings to His storehouse for His work in the World.

PRAYER: Heavenly Father, we may not understand the "why" of all You teach, but we cannot doubt the wisdom of it, or its good purpose. And so, with confidence in Your ways, we bring our gifts to You today through Jesus Christ, our Lord. Amen.

MALACHI 3:10

Bring ye all the tithes into the storehouse, that there may be meat in mine house, and prove me now herewith, saith the Lord of hosts, if I will not open you the windows of heaven, and pour you out a blessing, that there shall not be room enough to receive it.

"Bring ye all the tithes into the storehouse, that there may be food in mine house, and test me now herewith, saith the Lord of hosts, if I will not open for you the windows of heaven, and pour out for you a blessing, that there shall not be room enough to receive it."

God invites you to test Him in the matter of giving. Can you afford to give? How much can you afford to give? God invites you to test Him on the basis of the tithe.

If you can trust God for salvation, surely you can trust Him for your earthly needs; if you can believe His word for eternity, you can surely believe it for time.

Let us respond to God's invitation as we worship Him with our tithes and offerings.

PRAYER: Heavenly Father, thank You for Your promises to supply all the needs for soul and body. Forgive us for fears of our own security that keep us from giving to You for the spiritual need of others as we ought. In faith and love we give this proportion this morning. Use it to bring Your promises to others, we pray in Jesus' name. Amen.

Bring ye all the tithes into the storehouse, that there may be meat in mine house, and prove me now herewith, saith the Lord of hosts, if I will not open you the windows of heaven, and pour you out a blessing, that there shall not be room enough to receive it.

"Bring ye all the tithes into the storehouse, that there may be food in mine house, and prove me now herewith, saith the Lord of hosts, if I will not open for you the windows of heaven, and pour out for you a blessing, that there shall not be room enough to receive it."

We are not Bible-believing Christians just because we have Bible-based teachings. Unless we live our lives day by day according to the ways set forth in the Bible, with confidence that God will care for us as He promises in the Bible, we are not really Bible believers.

In respect to giving, we are not really Bible believers unless we give to meet the needs of others, confident that God will then supply our needs according to His promise.

Let us give as Bible-believing Christians as we worship the Lord with our systematic, proportionate gifts.

PRAYER: Heavenly Father, You are most surely worthy of our trust in all things. May we exercise that trust, not only for our salvation, but also for our sustenance, and thereby meet the spiritual needs of others through the gifts we offer today in the name of our Lord, Jesus Christ. Amen.

MALACHI 3:10

Bring ye all the tithes into the storehouse, that there may be meat in mine house, and prove me now herewith, saith the Lord of hosts, if I will not open you the windows of heaven, and pour you out a blessing, that there shall not be room enough to receive it.

A letter from one of our missionaries says, "Tithing has not always been a part of my life. I remember our pastor gave a series of sermons on giving. The thing that really impressed me—in fact, socked me squarely between my spiritual eyes—was when he emphasized that all my income was a gift from the Lord, and that instead of thinking how much I should give to Him, I should be thinking how much He wants me to keep for my needs. It all belongs to Him.

"I began tithing my net income. Then we began tithing our gross salary. Since then we have been praying that the Lord would increase our faith to give an increasing percentage of our income. He has allowed us to approach 20 percent of our income.

"But the amount is not the important thing to us now. The important thing is the increase in our faith as we look more and more to the Lord to provide our needs and to trust Him in our giving, even when there are great financial needs facing us."

This is the grace of giving; this is giving not grudgingly or of necessity. This is the key to prosperity: "Bring all your tithes . . . and I will pour out a blessing you cannot contain" (Malachi 3:10).

In that spirit and grace let us worship the Lord with our systematic, proportionate giving.

PRAYER: Heavenly Father, thank You for all You give us, spiritually and materially. Thank You for working in our hearts to give. Thank You for supplying all our needs. May our giving today show how much we really trust You. In Jesus' name, Amen.

Lay not up for yourselves treasures upon earth, where moth and rust doth corrupt, and where thieves break through and steal: but lay up for yourselves treasures in heaven, where neither moth nor rust doth corrupt, and where thieves do not break through and steal.

Jesus said, "Lay not up for yourselves treasures upon earth, where moth and rust doth corrupt, and where thieves break through and steal, but lay up for yourselves treasures in heaven, where neither moth nor rust doth corrupt, and where thieves do not break through nor steal; for where your treasure is, there will your heart be also."

Some people wonder why God never becomes very real to them. Perhaps the reason is to be found in their giving habits.

We may believe ever so strongly in God, and be ever so faithful in church attendance, Bible reading, and prayer, but if most of our substance is used for self, self will be the real and big thing in our life, and God will not be very real.

Start investing a larger part in His work by sharing His concern for the lost and see how this helps to make Him real in your life.

He is real to those who worship Him with their treasures.

PRAYER: Heavenly Father, when we remember that all that is in the world shall pass away, and that those who try to satisfy themselves with the things of this life will only thirst again, we realize we ought to bind ourselves and our substance to Thee. May we give enough today that our hearts will be drawn to Thee. In Jesus' name, Amen.

MATTHEW 6:20-21

Lay not up for yourselves treasures upon earth, where moth and rust doth corrupt, and where thieves break through and steal: but lay up for yourselves treasures in heaven, where neither moth nor rust doth corrupt, and where thieves do not break through and steal. For where your treasure is, there will your heart be also.

Jesus said: "Lay up for yourselves treasures in heaven . . . for where your treasure is, there will your heart be also."

Giving is a spiritual thermometer. The proportion of our giving is an indication of the proportion of our faith and of the proportion of our grateful dedication.

As we learn to honor God with our systematic, proportionate giving, we will find our faith strengthened in all areas and our dedication deepened.

May our spiritual thermometer register high as we worship the Lord with our treasures today.

PRAYER: Heavenly Father, teach us that true values are found in things eternal. Help us to trust You for present needs as we dedicate all our substance to You, to give as You direct. May our hearts be warm toward You as we give today through Jesus Christ, our Lord. Amen.

MATTHEW 6:33

But seek ye first the kingdom of God, and his righteousness; and all these things shall be added unto you.

"Seek ye first the kingdom of God, and his righteousness and all these things shall be added unto you."

God knows you have need of "these things." And He will give you these things. He only asks that you put Him first—in your values—in your effort—in your stewardship of substance.

Let us put God first as we worship Him with our tithes and offerings (taken out first from our paychecks).

PRAYER: Heavenly Father, with thanksgiving for past blessings received, and confidence in Your care and provision for the future, we bring You our love gifts this morning. We are not worthy to offer them, but offer them through our Lord, Jesus Christ. May other people be helped through them. Amen.

But seek ye first the kingdom of God, and his righteousness; and all these things shall be added unto you.

A sign in a grocery store said, "Pay your grocer first; you need him most." If the logic of this is convincing, it is well to ask, "Who do I need most?"

My answer would be "God." But when we pay the grocer first, and all our other bills, and give God out of what is left; when we say, "I must take care of my bills and can't afford to give," we are saying, "I don't need God as much as I need the businessman. God won't help me as much as the merchant."

Underlying this, is there not a basic lack of trust that God is concerned with our material needs, as well as our spiritual needs? But God says in Matthew 6:33, "Seek ye first the kingdom of God, and his righteousness, and all these things shall be added unto you."

On the basis of this promise let us worship the Lord with the first fruits of our increase.

PRAYER: Heavenly Father, we are so thankful for Your concern for our everyday needs, and Your provision of them. We would show our gratitude and our trust by giving You the first part of our income to be used in Your work here and abroad. May the needs of Your work be fully met as we trustfully give, through Jesus, our Lord. Amen.

MATTHEW 6:33

But seek ye first the kingdom of God, and his righteousness; and all these things shall be added unto you.

"Seek ye first the kingdom of God, and his righteousness, and all these things shall be added unto you."

Some Christians give less than they could because they want to be sure they have enough for tomorrow. Animals don't worry about tomorrow. Of course, they can't think about tomorrow, but neither can they have faith in God.

Christians can think about tomorrow, and they can also know that our Heavenly Father watches over us, and can trust Him to keep His promises and provide all our needs.

Let us seek first the kingdom of God and His righteousness and trust Him to supply our needs as we worship the Lord by putting Him first in our budget.

PRAYER: Heavenly Father, we thank Thee for Thy faithfulness in supplying our every need, and Thy generosity in doing it. Now may we be generous in our gifts to Thee as we trust Thee for all our needs. In the name of our Savior, Amen.

MATTHEW 9:36

But when he saw the multitudes, he was moved with compassion on them, because they fainted, and were scattered abroad, as sheep having no shepherd.

"When Jesus saw the multitudes, He was moved with compassion for them, because they . . . were as sheep having no shepherd."

Week after week we give for the preaching of the gospel. Is there no end to it?

Not while there are more people without the gospel than when we became Christians; not while there are seventy million more people every year to reach with the gospel; not while two thousand language groups have no Word of God in their own tongue; not while the love of God for a lost world is shed abroad in our hearts.

As long as God supplies our daily needs we are bound to give for others, systematically and proportionately.

Again today, then, let us be good stewards of the manifold grace of God.

PRAYER: Heavenly Father, we would not shut up our hearts of compassion, or become weary in well-doing. With joy we receive our weekly income. With joy may we give a portion for those who need to know You. By our gifts today may some hear the gospel and be saved, through Jesus Christ, our Lord. Amen.

MATTHEW 10:8

Heal the sick, cleanse the lepers, raise the dead, cast out devils: freely ye have received, freely give.

"Freely ye have received, freely give."

As we were growing up, others provided a church for us, the gospel was preached to us without charge, and we received eternal life as the gift of God. Truly we have received freely.

Now we have a chance to provide for others—a church, the gospel, and eternal life—in this community and around the world, as we worship the Lord with our systematic, proportionate gifts, freely given.

PRAYER: Heavenly Father, we thank Thee for Thy Gift, and for those who gave that we might have the Gift. Now may we freely give that others may likewise be blessed. May these gifts we offer this morning bring eternal life to many, through Jesus Christ, our Lord. Amen.

And when they were come to Capernaum, they that received tribute money came to Peter, and said, Doth not your master pay tribute? He saith, Yes. And when he was come into the house, Jesus prevented him, saying, What thinkest thou, Simon? of whom do the kings of the earth take custom or tribute? of their own children, or of strangers? Peter saith unto him, Of strangers. Jesus saith unto him, Then are the children free. Notwithstanding, lest we should offend them, go thou to the sea, and cast an hook, and take up the fish that first cometh up; and when thou hast opened his mouth, thou shalt find a piece of money: that take, and give unto them for me and thee.

Did you realize that Jesus was a tither? Doubtless, during the early years when He worked in the carpenter shop, He faithfully practiced God's principle of systematic and proportionate giving, taking the tithes out first to give to the Lord.

And He said to others, concerning the tithe, "This ought ye to do" (Matthew 23:23). When men asked His disciples, "Does not your Master pay the temple tax?" they said Yes.

In this matter too, then, He becomes our example, that we should follow in His steps.

Let us follow His example as we worship the Lord with our tithes and offerings.

PRAYER: Heavenly Father, thank You for the example of Jesus. Like Him, we would fulfill all righteousness. We bring Your tithe today and offer it through the merit of Jesus, our Savior. Amen.

MATTHEW 22:20-21
(Taxes)

And he saith unto them, Whose is this image and superscription? They say unto him, Caesar's. Then saith he unto them, Render therefore unto Caesar the things which are Caesar's, and unto God the things that are God's.

It will soon be April 15th and everyone is working to get their income tax in on time. This brings forcefully to our minds the words of Jesus, "Render unto Caesar the things which are Caesar's and unto God, the things that are God's."

He would have us be very careful to pay our taxes and all other obligations to the state, and to do it on time. He would have us be just as careful in giving to God that which is right.

As Uncle Sam will not permit us to withhold more than we should, so, too, it will be found that God's dealings with us are measured partly in terms of our giving and withholding.

We pay our taxes. Now let us worship the Lord with our systematic, proportionate giving.

PRAYER: Heavenly Father, we are very careful to render to our government what is required, partly out of gratitude for the benefits we receive, perhaps partly out of fear. Teach us to be careful to give to You what You expect of us, systematically, proportionately, out of gratitude and a wholesome respect for You as God. In Jesus' name. Amen.

MATTHEW 22:20-21
(Taxes)

And he saith unto them, Whose is this image and superscription? They say unto him, Caesar's. Then saith he unto them, Render therefore unto Caesar the things which are Caesar's; and unto God the things that are God's.

Jesus said, "Render unto Caesar the things which are Caesar's; and unto God, the things that are God's."

There is a difference: Caesar compels; God invites. Yet we ought to do it. There is a clear implication that some of our things belong to Caesar, and thus we must pay them. There is an equally clear implication that some of our things belong to God and thus we ought to give them to Him.

God expects it; He requires it. But He does not compel. Will we then fail to recognize His rights?

Just as taxes are taken out first, before we spend the rest, let us honor God with our first fruits as we worship Him with our tithes and offerings.

PRAYER: Heavenly Father, let us hide our faces in shame if we only do for You what we have to do. We recognize that all we have comes from You and we want to give back part of it. May it accomplish something of eternal worth in other lives as we offer it through Jesus Christ, our Lord. Amen.

MATTHEW 22:20-21
(Taxes)

And he saith unto them, Whose is this image and superscription? They say unto him, Caesar's. Then saith he unto them, Render therefore unto Caesar the things which are Caesar's; and unto God the things that are God's.

"Render unto Caesar the things which are Caesar's; and unto God, the things that are God's."

Most Christians render unto Caesar the things which are Caesar's—pay their taxes—because if they don't they get called in to give an account, and they have to pay a fine beside.

If we fail to render unto God the things that are God's, we will also be called in to give an account.

"We must all appear before the judgment seat of Christ, that every one may receive . . . according to that he hath done, whether it be good or bad" (II Corinthians 5:10).

Let us give as those who will give account, as we worship the Lord with His tithes and our offerings.

PRAYER: Heavenly Father, may we not presume on Thy grace by neglecting to give as we ought. Rather, may the fear of the Lord and the love of the Lord combine to make us honest in our dealings with Thee as we give. Inspect our gifts today and correct us if they are not suitable. In Jesus' name we pray. Amen.

MATTHEW 23:23

Woe unto you, scribes and Pharisees, hypocrites! for ye pay tithe of mint and anise and cummin, and have omitted the weightier matters of the law, judgment, mercy, and faith: these ought ye to have done, and not to leave the other undone.

Jesus said, "Woe unto you, scribes and Pharisees, hypocrites! you pay tithes . . . and have omitted the weightier matters of the Law—judgment and mercy and faithfulness. These ought you to have done, and not to leave the other undone."

It is wrong to think to buy ourselves off from other responsibilities toward God by generous gifts in the offering plate; we cannot substitute one obligation for another.

On the other hand, it is wrong to excuse ourselves from giving our substance because we give our time. We ought to do both, He says.

Let us fulfill all that God expects, as we worship Him with our systematic, proportionate giving.

PRAYER: Heavenly Father, deliver us from covetousness, from disobedience, and from excuses. Whatever else we are doing for You, this morning it is our joyful duty to bring these offerings for Your use in other lives, through Jesus Christ, our Lord. Amen.

For whosoever will save his life shall lose it; but whosoever shall lose his life for my sake and the gospel's, the same shall save it.

A man who was in debt for a large sum of money was approached by a friend who said, "Now aren't you sorry you gave so much to the Lord?" "No," he said, "I am glad, for that is the only investment I made that is still paying dividends."

Jesus said, "He that saveth his life shall lose it; he that loseth his life [and his substance] for my sake and the gospel's, shall save it" (Mark 8:35)

How true this is. The most lasting investment we can make of our substance is to put it at the Lord's disposal for His use. Let us invest well as we worship the Lord with our systematic, proportionate giving.

PRAYER: Heavenly Father, we thank You we can lay up treasure in heaven; that You have given us the substance and the privilege of investing some of it in eternal causes. Guide us in our giving. Help us to lay up treasure in that place where it is not destroyed, through Jesus Christ. Amen.

MARK 12:17
(Taxes)

And Jesus answering said unto them, Render to Caesar the things that are Caesar's and to God the things that are God's. And they marvelled at him.

Jesus said, "Render to Caesar the things that are Ceasar's, and to God the things that are God's."

At this time of the year many are thinking about paying their income taxes. These are not voluntary, but compulsory, and we ought to pay them in full—honestly. But this country is only the place of our earthly citizenship.

But Christ is King as well as Savior, and our true and abiding citizenship is in heaven. Then how much more ought we willingly to offer gifts to Him for the work of His kingdom!

And just as that which we render to Caesar is proportionate, so ought that be which we render to God.

Think of it: our Sovereign, omnipotent King does not compel, but invites us to give. Can we do less than we do for our earthly citizenship?

Freely ye have received. Freely give, as we worship the Lord with the things that are His.

PRAYER: Heavenly Father, may our giving today acknowledge Your Lordship, Your sovereign majesty; and just as our taxes are for benefits received, so may our giving acknowledge our debt to grace for all the benefits we have received through Jesus Christ, our Lord. Amen.

MARK 14:3-9

And being in Bethany in the house of Simon the leper, as he sat at meat, there came a woman having an alabaster box of ointment of spikenard very precious; and she brake the box, and poured it on his head. And there were some that had indignation within themselves, and said, Why was this waste of the ointment made? For it might have been sold for more than three hundred pence, and have been given to the poor. And they murmured against her. And Jesus said, Let her alone; why trouble ye her? she hath wrought a good work on me. For ye have the poor with you always, and whensoever ye will ye may do them good; but me ye have not always. She hath done what she could: she is come aforehand to anoint my body to the burying.

When Mary wanted to show love and devotion to Jesus, it was either all or nothing. She could not remove a stopper and pour out a little perfume. She had to break the flask and give it all to Him.

Her decision received the commendation of Jesus.

If we would express our love and devotion, we will not be doling out a little when the collection is taken, but will give all we have to Him and use it as He directs.

Let our giving this morning be an act of loving devotion to Him.

PRAYER: Heavenly Father, with the same freedom and joy that we spend for those we love, we give to Thee now. All we are and have is because of Thy grace, and we are grateful. We want our offerings to be worthy of Thy commendation, as we present them through the One who gave Himself for us. Amen.

MARK 16:15
(Missionary Sunday)

And he said unto them, Go ye into all the world, and preach the gospel to every creature.

Jesus said, "Go ye into all the world and preach the gospel to every creature." Although there *is* a missionary aspect to the work we are doing in our own neighborhood, a lot of what we give is for the benefit of ourselves and our own families. But God is interested in the whole world, and He is concerned for those who have not heard. "To every creature" must ever be in the forefront of our thinking.

Let us share His concern for others, as we worship the Lord with our systematic, proportionate giving.

PRAYER: Heavenly Father, help us to lift up our eyes and see our fellowmen as lost, without God and without hope. Then may we give in a measure that will make it possible for them to hear Your gospel. In Jesus' name. Amen.

MARK 16:15
(Missionary Sunday)

And he said unto them, Go ye into all the world, and preach the gospel to every creature.

"Go ye into all the world and preach the gospel to every creature."

If you are sure God has not called you to go to the foreign field, you may be equally sure He has called you to give so others can go. It is our responsibility, either by work or by substance, to see that all have a chance to hear.

Let us worship the Lord with our systematic, proportionate giving, so that all may know Him.

PRAYER: Heavenly Father, we are glad for our salvation. Give us a genuine concern for the salvation of others. Thank You for loving the whole world. Help us to love them too. Use our offerings today to bring eternal life to others, through Jesus Christ our Savior, in whose name we bring them. Amen.

MARK 16:15
(Missionary Sunday)

And he said unto them, Go ye into all the world, and preach the gospel to every creature.

Jesus said, "Go ye into all the world, and preach the gospel to every creature."

If we do not go in person, we sense we should be giving to send someone else. And the need for giving will not be done until the gospel has been preached to every creature. The more adequately we give, the more people of our own generation will hear the gospel. Let no one be deprived of heaven because we keep back more than we should.

Let us give with this purpose as we worship the Lord with systematic, proportionate giving.

PRAYER: Heavenly Father, thank You that salvation is a gift. But may we not receive the gift, and then be indifferent to the need of others to hear about the gift. Give us a strong sense of responsibility to those without God and without hope in this world, that we might give as we should. Judge these gifts we bring this morning through our Savior. Amen.

LUKE 2:32
(Christmas)

A light to lighten the Gentiles, and the glory of thy people Israel.

When Jesus was born, His parents brought Him to the Temple, and Simeon said, He is "a light to lighten the Gentiles."

Each month each of us receives a light bill. It always hurts a little to pay it, but who would rather live in the dark? We could, but we choose not to, and we are willing to pay the light bill.

At Christmas time we use even more light, knowing the bill will go up; but we would not want to celebrate the coming of the Savior without light. And so we let the light shine and pay the bill.

There is a gospel light bill, too. Because someone paid it in years past, we live in the light of the gospel instead of in spiritual darkness. Now it is our privilege to pay it for someone else. We could let them live in darkness, but do we really want that?

Our offering will give the answer, as we worship the Lord with gifts for the Light of the world.

PRAYER: Heavenly Father, thank You for Jesus, whose life is the light of men, that we might not walk in darkness. In His name we give today, that His light may shine farther, even to the uttermost part of the earth, as well as here at home. Amen.

Give, and it shall be given unto you; good measure, pressed down, and shaken together, and running over, shall men give into your bosom. For with the same measure that ye mete withal it shall be measured to you again.

We were not given life in order that God might honor us, but that we might honor Him. This is true in our living and in our giving. We do not give to get from God, but to honor God. And we can do this best with systematic, proportionate giving—a definite percentage of our income given to the Lord to honor Him who is the source of all we have.

And then, grace upon grace, we find that it is His delight to honor those who honor Him. He will not have any man be poorer by giving. Many verses may be summed up in this one in Luke 6:38, "Give, and it shall be given unto you."

With pure motive, let us so give that we may honor God.

PRAYER: Heavenly Father, Your ways with us are marvelous indeed. We have given time and again without suffering need. We have found You faithful to Your promise to supply our needs when we supply the needs of others, especially of those who are in the work of the gospel. It is our delight to honor You today with our gifts. May they be of adequate measure to do this, as we offer them through our Lord, Jesus Christ. Amen.

Give, and it shall be given unto you; good measure, pressed down, and shaken together, and running over, shall men give into your bosom. For with the same measure that ye mete withal it shall be measured to you again.

Why should we give? There are several reasons.

1. Because all we have comes *from* the Lord. "Every good gift is from above."

2. Because all we have *is* the Lord's. "All things come of thee, O Lord, and of thine own have we given thee."

3. Because He claims a certain portion for Himself. "The tithe is the Lord's."

4. Because Christians should have the mind of Christ, a mind for others. "Let this mind be in you, which was also in Christ Jesus." His love in our hearts should keep us from being selfish.

5. Because He promises to give to those who give. "Give, and it will be given to you; good measure, pressed down, shaken together, running over, shall men give to you. For with the same measure you give it shall be given to you again."

For all these reasons, let us worship the Lord with our systematic, proportionate giving.

PRAYER: *Heavenly Father, when our natural selfishness suggests many reasons why we should not give, may Your reasons why we should give win the battle. For all these reasons we present our offerings today in the merit of our Lord, Jesus Christ. Amen.*

LUKE 7:47
(Thanksgiving)

Wherefore I say unto thee, Her sins, which are many, are forgiven; for she loved much: but to whom little is forgiven the same loveth little.

Thanksgiving is not only a time for saying thanks, which is always polite; it is a time for showing that we are thankful. Giving thanks centers on the gift. Being thankful centers on the Giver and prompts us to bring Him not only words but something more tangible.

As thankful people we demonstrate with our offerings our love for God who first loved us, and has done so much for us. "To whom much is forgiven, the same loves much" (Luke 7:47).

Let us worship the Lord with a "great love offering" this morning.

PRAYER: *HeavenlyFather, we are thankful that You spared not Your Son, but delivered Him up for us all, and with Him have freely given us all things. Now we would show our love by the offering we bring today, to be used in Your service, through Jesus Christ, our Redeemer and Lord. Amen.*

LUKE 7:47

Wherefore I say unto thee, Her sins, which are many, are forgiven; for she loved much: but to whom little is forgiven, the same loveth little.

A missionary intern called in the home of an elderly man and led him to the Lord. Afterward the man said, "I haven't much, but I am so happy I want to give something for the Lord," and he handed over a five-dollar roll of dimes.

This is the natural response of every heart who realizes what it means to be saved. To adapt a word from Jesus, "To whom much is forgiven, the same loveth much" (Luke 7:47).

From forgiven and loving hearts let us present our tithes and offerings to the Lord.

PRAYER: Heavenly Father, thank You for Your forgiveness. We have been forgiven much. We love You much. We are glad for the opportunity to give. Use our gifts to bring forgiveness to others as we offer them through Jesus, our Savior. Amen.

LUKE 8:2-3

And certain women, which had been healed of evil spirits and infirmities . . . ministered unto him of their substance.

Luke 8:2-3 says, "Certain women who had been healed of evil spirits and infirmities . . . ministered unto [Jesus] of their substance."

They had received spiritual help from Jesus; gladly they gave of their substance for His material help—both of their substance and service. The one does not relieve a person of the responsibility to do the other.

He deigned to be supported that way in the preaching of the Gospel—and He still does so today.

Let us minister to Jesus with our substance, in response to His grace in our lives.

PRAYER: Heavenly Father, how wonderfully You have healed us of our evil spirits and helped us with our weaknesses and needs. Now we gladly would minister to You today with our substance and service. Bless these gifts as You have already blessed us, we pray in Jesus' name. Amen.

A certain man went down from Jerusalem to Jericho, and fell among thieves, which stripped him of his raiment, and wounded him, and departed, leaving him half dead. And by chance there came down a certain priest that way: and when he saw him, he passed by on the other side. And likewise a Levite, when he was at the place, came and looked on him, and passed by on the other side. But a certain Samaritan, as he journeyed, came where he was: and when he saw him, he had compassion on him, and went to him, and bound up his wounds, pouring in oil and wine, and set him on his own beast, and brought him to an inn, and took care of him. And on the morrow when he departed, he took out two pence, and gave them to the host, and said unto him, Take care of him; and whatsoever thou spendest more, when I come again, I will repay thee.

In the story of the Good Samaritan we meet four kinds of people: the thieves who took what belonged to others for themselves, the priest and Levite who kept what they had for themselves, the Good Samaritan who shared what he had, and the man in need.

If, as Jesus said, "it is more blessed to give than to receive," it is not hard to know which of the four was the more blessed.

Let us all be Good Samaritans toward a world in need, as we worship the Lord by sharing what we have with others.

PRAYER: *Heavenly Father, thank You for the Good Samaritans in this world. May we be a part of their company every day—our eyes open to see, our hearts open to care, and our pocketbooks open to help. We are glad we can give today, through Jesus Christ, our Lord. Amen.*

LUKE 10:33

But a certain Samaritan, as he journeyed, came where he was: and when he saw him, he had compassion on him.

The good Samaritan was no more obligated than the rest of those who passed by a wounded man, but he was constrained by love for his neighbor. He was interested in and concerned for anybody whose need he recognized.

Therefore, out of his own pocket he provided for the man's need; and left word that as long as the need continued he would continue to give.

There are many material needs in the world; there are even more spiritual needs. May the love of God which is poured out in our hearts by the Holy Spirit make us interested in and actively concerned for all whose needs we recognize, both here and abroad; and thus may we continue to give to our local work and our worldwide ministry, as we worship the Lord with our systematic proportionate offerings.

PRAYER: Heavenly Father, we are naturally selfish. Thank You for putting love for others in our hearts. May we not stifle that with our selfishness, but let it overcome our selfishness so we cheerfully give to help others in their need. Bless the offering we bring this morning to the needs of others, we pray in Jesus' name. Amen.

LUKE 10:37

And he said, He that shewed mercy on him. Then said Jesus unto him, Go, and do thou likewise.

The story of the Good Samaritan ends with these words, "Go, and do thou likewise." The point of that story was that a man voluntarily shared what he had with others. And the conclusion was, "Go, and do thou likewise."

The love of God in our hearts will prompt us to do so as we worship the Lord with our systematic, proportionate giving.

PRAYER: Heavenly Father, overcome the covetousness and selfishness within us, so that instead of taking what belongs to others, or keeping what we have for ourselves, we might share what we have with others in their need. May the gifts we bring this morning be acceptable in Thy sight, through Jesus Christ, our Lord. Amen.

And I will say to my soul, Soul, thou hast much goods laid up for many years; take thine ease, eat, drink, and be merry. But God said unto him, Thou fool, this night thy soul shall be required of thee: then whose shall those things be, which thou hast provided?

When Jesus told of the rich man who put his surplus in storage and said, "Eat, drink and be merry," God said, "Thou fool!" And we agree! And then Jesus added, "So is everyone that lays up treasure for himself, and is not rich toward God."

There is a better thing to do with money than spend or save it all. It is to give some to the Lord and His work. God promises it will bring blessing here and hereafter.

Let us be rich toward God as we worship Him with our treasure.

PRAYER: Heavenly Father, it is so natural for us to work to get, and then to spend it on ourselves, now or later. Work in us to overcome that, and help us to grow in the grace of giving. Bless other people with that which we offer today through the merit of our Savior, Jesus. Amen.

LUKE 14:12-14

Then said he also to him that bade him, When thou makest a dinner or a supper, call not thy friends, nor thy brethren, neither thy kinsmen, nor thy rich neighbours; lest they also bid thee again, and a recompence be made thee. But when thou makest a feast, call the poor, the maimed, the lame, the blind: And thou shalt be blessed; for they cannot recompense thee; for thou shalt be recompensed at the resurrection of the just.

To a man who invited Him to dinner, Jesus said, "When you invite folk for dinner, don't invite your friends, or relatives, or well-to-do neighbors, lest they also invite you to a dinner and you are thereby rewarded. But invite the poor, the lame, and the blind, and you will be blessed, for they cannot reward you, but you shall be rewarded at the resurrection of the just."

The lesson here is that true giving is not a scheme to advance our interests or bring us a return, but to meet the needs of others; not with the thought of what it will do for us, but what it will do for the other person.

Let us engage in the kind of giving God takes note of and will reward as we worship the Lord with our systematic, proportionate gifts.

PRAYER: Heavenly Father, what can You gain from Your great gift to us?—We have nothing to bless You with. Then may we give in that same spirit today, through Jesus Christ, our Lord. Amen.

LUKE 16:11

If therefore ye have not been faithful in the unrighteous mammon, who will commit to your trust the true riches?

Jesus said, "If you are not faithful in your stewardship of money matters, who will commit to your trust the true riches"—spiritual treasures and the opportunity to serve the Lord?

That is, if we cannot recognize God's Lordship over our material possessions, He will not trust us with far greater and abiding riches.

In faithful stewardship, then, let us worship the Lord with our systematic, proportionate giving, that we might have greater spiritual treasure and opportunity.

PRAYER: Heavenly Father, help us to understand that giving for Christians is not an option, but a responsibility; that we have an obligation to see that a right portion of our material substance is invested for eternal dividends, in the service of Christ, through whom we offer these gifts this morning. Amen.

JOHN 3:16

For God so loved the world, that he gave his only begotten Son, that whosoever believeth in him should not perish, but have everlasting life.

"God so loved the world that he gave."

You may give without loving, but you won't love without giving.

And when love gives, it is not grudgingly or of necessity; it delights to do so, and only wishes it could do more. That's why God loves a cheerful giver—it's a sign of love.

Let us worship God with our offerings as those who love Him and His Son, our Savior.

PRAYER: Heavenly Father, we do love You and we pray for a love for all mankind—the kind of love that will prompt us to get involved with their needs, to which we give today, in Jesus' name. Amen.

ACTS 2:44-45

And all that believed were together, and had all things common; and sold their possessions and goods, and parted them to all men, as every man had need.

One of the interesting things the early Christians did voluntarily after Pentecost was to stop hoarding and start sharing. What they had to hoard was probably not much, but the principle was wrong. There were others with less than they. When the Spirit of Christ moves His people to be like Him, they always find the desire and the ability to share.

Acts 2:44-45 says, "All that believed were together, and had all things common; and sold their possessions and goods, and parted them to all, as every man had need."

With this God-given desire to share, let us worship the Lord with our possessions.

PRAYER: Heavenly Father, may Thy Spirit work in our hearts to overcome out natural selfishness and fear of the future, and give us instead a spirit of trust and concern for others, to whose welfare we dedicate these gifts this morning, through Jesus Christ, our Lord. Amen.

ACTS 4:32

And the multitude of them that believed were of one heart and of one soul: neither said any of them that ought of the things which he possessed was his own; but they had all things common.

It is said of the early Christians in Acts 4:32, "Neither said any of them that any thing he possessed was his own." Becoming a Christian changes a person's sense of relationship to his material possessions. He recognizes that he holds them in trust, and he desires to share with others in need.

Let us be sure that we are wholly Christian, including our attitude toward our material things. May our possessions be placed at the Lord's disposal, as we worship Him with our tithes and offerings.

PRAYER: Heavenly Father, thank You for saving our souls. Save our pocketbooks, too. May we count nothing our own—our time, our talents, our substance—but just hold them in trust to be used as You direct. In such a spirit we bring our gifts today, through Jesus Christ. Amen.

And the multitude of them that believed were of one heart and of one soul: neither said any of them that ought of the things which he possessed was his own; but they had all things common.

In the early church, the needs of some Christians were so great that other Christians sold their property to get cash to meet these needs. They were not compelled to do this; they wanted to because they had a Christian concern for others, and did not consider anything they had their own, but the Lord's.

This spirit and attitude today would be a long step toward bringing the revival, the power, and the testimony the church needs in the world.

On such a basis, let us worship the Lord with our systematic, proportionate giving.

PRAYER: Heavenly Father, we thank you for the opportunity to support ourselves, and that we even have some left over. May the world's needs be felt by us, and may we follow Your direction in giving to meet those needs. Encourage others through our giving today, we pray in Jesus' name. Amen.

ACTS 5:1-11

But a certain man named Ananias, with Sapphira his wife, sold a possession, and kept back part of the price, his wife also being privy to it, and brought a certain part, and laid it at the apostles' feet. But Peter said, Ananias, why hath Satan filled thine heart to lie to the Holy Ghost . . . ?

Because other people in the church were giving, Ananias and Sapphira thought they should give something too—they didn't want to appear less spiritual than the others.

They didn't give as much as they could, but they *pretended* they did—because they wanted the people to think they were spiritual.

Rightly, they equated giving with spirituality; wrongly they made giving a substitute for spirituality and God was displeased with them.

"Every man according as he purposeth in his heart, so let him give, not grudgingly, or of necessity; for God loveth a cheerful giver" (II Corinthians 9:7).

Let our giving this morning be from the heart as we worship the Lord with our systematic, proportionate giving.

PRAYER: Heavenly Father, help us to give today, not to impress giving people, but to help needy people. May Your love and concern for people have free course in our hearts to make us happy to give in proper measure, as you have prospered us, through Jesus Christ, our Lord. Amen.

ACTS 20:35
(Christmas)

I have shewed you all things, how that so labouring ye ought to support the weak, and to remember the words of the Lord Jesus, how he said, It is more blessed to give than to receive.

"Remember the words of the Lord Jesus, how he said, it is more blessed to give than to receive."

There are three stages in enjoying Christmas.

As children we learn that it is a time of receiving gifts, and this is lots of fun.

As young people we learn that it is a time of exchanging gifts, and this is fun too.

But we have not truly learned what fun Christmas is until we have learned that it is a time of giving gifts. Giving to help others in need, especially in spiritual need, is the real spirit of Christmas.

In the measure that we really give at Christmas—not just *swap*— we will know the true blessedness, for "it is more blessed to give than to receive."

In this spirit let us worship the Lord with our tithes and offerings.

PRAYER: Heavenly Father, Your Gift that first Christmas was not in response to any good thing we had given You, but only in response to our need, prompted by Your unmerited love for us. May the same be true of us in all of our giving, and in these offerings we bring You today through Your gift, the Lord Jesus. Amen.

I have shewed you all things, how that so labouring ye ought to support the weak, and to remember the words of the Lord Jesus, how he said, It is more blessed to give than to receive.

Jesus said, "It is more blessed to give than to receive."

The Sea of Galilee is surrounded by grass, trees, parks, animals and birds, and by people who come there to play. The Dead Sea, which receives its water from the same source and in the same amount, is surrounded by wasteland occupied by no living thing. People go there only out of curiosity. What is the reason for this difference? Galilee gives as it receives; the Dead Sea keeps what it receives.

This is a parable of life: keep and become a Scrooge, friendless and barren; give and be a happy and full person. It is indeed "more blessed to give than to receive."

Let us get in on the blessedness as we worship the Lord with our giving.

PRAYER: Heavenly Father, we thank Thee for all the good things we enjoy and which we have received from Thee. Let us not be selfish with them. Teach us to share them; to give with hearts of love and concern. Here are our gifts. May they be acceptable in Thy sight, and blessed to many other lives through Jesus, our Lord. Amen.

I have shewed you all things, how that so labouring ye ought to support the weak, and to remember the words of the Lord Jesus, how he said, It is more blessed to give than to receive.

Jesus said, "It is more blessed to give than to receive."

Some people praise God for the church; and yet if all gave in the same proportion as they, there would be no church. They need to learn stewardship.

Some people give frequently—but not during vacation time or other special seasons. They need to learn the discipline of systematic giving.

Some start, sputter—and then quit when their own wants require all they have. They need to learn the grace of proportionate giving.

Some give systematically and proportionately. They carry the load and are blessed in their stewardship.

The more we learn the grace of giving, the more we will discover the blessedness of giving and the more good will be done for others, and for the Lord.

Let us discover this blessedness as we worship the Lord with our giving.

PRAYER: Heavenly Father, thank You for the gospel and the ministry of the church. We would be ashamed to receive all this through the giving of others and then not give in order that others might also hear and receive these blessings. Help us to not close our minds when we consider how much we can give. Help us to grow in the grace of giving. Guide Your church in the use of these offerings we bring through Jesus Christ. Amen.

ROMANS 10:17
(Missionary Sunday)

So then faith cometh by hearing and hearing by the word of God.

"Faith cometh by hearing, and hearing by the Word of God."

The responsibility for preaching the gospel to every creature is the responsibility of every Christian.

We are not relieved of responsibility because we cannot *go*. It then becomes our responsibility to *send*—by giving. And we do not discharge our responsibility by giving what we can *spare*.

In true Christian discipleship, we dedicate our all to the Lord and retain for our own use only that which is right in the light of our world responsibility.

For the sake of a world without the Word of God, let us responsibly worship the Lord with our proportionate gifts.

PRAYER: Heavenly Father, help us to see our giving not as charity but as a response to our responsibility to You and to a world without God and without hope. We would not seek to discharge our responsibility by token giving, but in proper proportion we bring our offerings to You today for Your use, in Jesus' name. Amen.

ROMANS 12:6-8

Having then gifts differing according to the grace that is given to us, whether prophecy, let us prophesy according to the proportion of faith; or ministry, let us wait on our ministering: or he that teacheth, on teaching; or he that exhorteth, on exhortation: he that giveth, let him do it with simplicity; he that ruleth, with diligence; he that sheweth mercy, with cheerfulness.

"Having gifts that differ according to the grace that is given to us, . . . he that giveth, let him do it with liberality" (ASV).

Many Christians, rich and poor, possess the gift of giving. This gift is the ability to earn and give for the advancement of God's work with such wisdom and cheerfulness that the recipients are blessed and strengthened by it.

Let us exercise the gift of giving as we worship the Lord with our liberality.

PRAYER: Heavenly Father, thank You for the ability to give to You and thereby meet the needs of people, especially their need of the gospel. May we count every gift an investment for eternity. May the whole portion of our offering today be given gladly, through Jesus Christ, our Lord. Amen.

ROMANS 12:8b

He that giveth, let him do it with simplicity.

Speaking of the gifts of the Holy Spirit to each believer, Romans 12:8 says, "He that gives, let him do it with a generous, unselfish motive."

Giving, then, is a spiritual gift which can be exercised by all believers, regardless of the amount they have to give.

Let us exercise this gift of the Holy Spirit as we worship the Lord with our generosity.

PRAYER: Heavenly Father, thank You for Your spiritual gifts by which we can give material gifts from the material gifts You have first given us. May our material gifts have a spiritual ministry to others as we offer them through our Lord, Jesus Christ. Amen.

ROMANS 12:8b

He that giveth, let him do it with simplicity.

"He that giveth, let him do it with simplicity—sincerity—free of pretense—without seeking anything for self"—that is, not to impress people or satisfy the church.

Your giving is between you and the Lord, motivated by His love and goodness toward you, and measured by your love for Him.

Let us thus worship the Lord with our sincere gifts.

PRAYER: Heavenly Father, we love You because You first loved us, and give to You because You first gave to us. May our love and our giving be an adequate response as we offer these gifts through Jesus Christ, our Lord. Amen.

Love worketh no ill to his neighbour: therefore love is the fulfilling of the law.

Christians are not under Law, but under grace; but the intent is that the righteousness of the Law be fulfilled in us, including the laws of stewardship and care for others. To put it another way, Romans 13:10 says, "Love is the fulfilling of the Law."

True conversion touches on our relationship to our possessions and to other people. We are not wholly converted until our giving is affected.

Let us be sure that our giving is Christian as we worship the Lord with our systematic, proportionate love gifts.

PRAYER: Heavenly Father, deliver us as Christians from selfishness and the fear of insecurity. Teach us to love others enough to be concerned about them and their needs, and to trust Thee for our own. Thus may we worship Thee aright with our giving today, and every Lord's day. In Jesus' name. Amen.

ROMANS 14:9

For to this end Christ both died, and rose, and revived, that he might be Lord both of the dead and living.

"To this end Christ both died and rose . . . that he might be Lord."

When we receive Christ as Savior, we acknowledge His right to direct both our living and our giving. Thus we should ever be seeking His guidance in both aspects of our life. Follow His guidance and you will find your own life blessed thereby.

May we follow His guidance as we worship Him now with our systematic proportion.

PRAYER: Heavenly Father, thank You for Christ who died and rose and gives us forgiveness and life and hope. Help us to acknowledge His Lordship in all aspects of our life, including our stewardship of substance. May our offerings today reflect that Lordship as we offer them through His merit. Amen.

I CORINTHIANS 4:2

Moreover it is required in stewards, that a man be found faithful.

The world says, "Get all you can." God's grace teaches us to give all we can, and even more—beyond our means.

The world says, "It is wonderful to get and have." God's Son teaches us that "it is more blessed to give than to receive."

The natural heart says, "Spend it on yourself or save it for a rainy day." God says, "Thy soul shall be required of thee; then whose shall these things be?" And again, "It is required in stewards that a man be found faithful."

With this sense of stewardship let us worship the Lord with our tithes and offerings.

PRAYER: Heavenly Father, we would overcome the wisdom and self-interest of man, and learn the grace of giving. Give us the mind of Christ for others; to go beyond what we feel we can afford, to bring the Savior to a world without God and without hope. To that end we present these offerings through Jesus. Amen.

I CORINTHIANS 9:11

If we have sown unto you spiritual things, is it a great thing if we reap your carnal things?

"If we have sown unto you spiritual things, is it a great thing if we shall reap your carnal things?" Paul asked the Corinthian church.

God counts it a small thing for us to give of our material blessings when we have received so bountifully of His spiritual blessings. And it is by sharing our material blessings that still others can know the spiritual blessings.

So let us not give sparingly, but bountifully as we worship God with our systematic, proportionate giving.

PRAYER: Heavenly Father, thank You for your blessings of grace: salvation, peace, joy, hope, and much more. May we not expect to have all these and keep all our material substance too, when it is only by our giving that others will know these gifts of Your grace. May gratitude impel us to give as we ought as we present, this morning, our tithes and offerings to You through Jesus Christ, our Lord. Amen.

I CORINTHIANS 15:58
(Easter)

Therefore, my beloved brethren, be ye stedfast, unmoveable, always abounding in the work of the Lord, forasmuch as ye know that your labour is not in vain in the Lord.

Having spoken of the resurrection, Paul said, "Therefore . . . always abound in the work of the Lord."

Much of that abounding must be in labor; some of it must be in giving, to cover things we ourselves cannot do and to send the resurrection message to places we cannot go.

If we give occasionally, but not always, obviously the need will not always be met. If we give, but do not abound in giving, obviously only part of the abounding needs will be met. It is as we "always abound" that the needs will be met and the work be accomplished.

From the inspiration of the resurrection, let us always abound as we worship the Lord with our proportionate giving.

PRAYER: Heavenly Father, thank You for Jesus, who died for our sins and rose for our justification, and who ever lives to intercede for us. Until His coming, we would give and give and give again, till the whole world knows. To this end we bring our offerings and pray Thy guidance and blessing in their use. In the name of our risen Lord. Amen.

I CORINTHIANS 15:58—16:2
(Easter)

Therefore, my beloved brethren, be ye stedfast, unmoveable, always abounding in the work of the Lord, forasmuch as ye know that your labour is not in vain in the Lord. Now concerning the collection for the saints, as I have given order to the churches of Galatia, even so do ye. Upon the first day of the week let every one of you lay by him in store, as God hath prospered him.

First Corinthians 15, that great chapter on the proof and meaning of the resurrection, closes with this statement, "therefore . . . be ye stedfast, unmovable, always abounding in the work of the Lord, forasmuch as ye know that your labour is not in vain in the Lord " (v. 58).

And chapter 16 opens with this statement, "Now concerning the collection . . . on the first day of the week let every one of you lay by him in store, as God has prospered him" (vv. 1-2).

Systematic, proportionate giving was practiced under the Law, but it is based on the resurrection. Those with resurrection joy and hope delight to honor the risen Christ, not only with their regular attendance at worship services on the first day of the week with praise on their lips, but with their substance, a part of themselves given in thanks to Him who gave Himself for them.

Let us truly worship our risen Lord today as God has prospered us.

PRAYER: Heavenly Father, thank You for sparing not Your Son, but delivering Him up for us all, and then raising Him again from the dead that we might have life, abundant and everlasting. May such love prompt us to give in love, and to love to give. We present our offerings today, not as a tax, but as a way of saying, "Thank You that Christ died for our sins and rose again." Help us to abound in such good works because they are not in vain. In Jesus' name. Amen.

I CORINTHIANS 16:1-2
(Easter)

Now concerning the collection for the saints, as I have given order to the churches of Galatia, even so do ye. Upon the first day of the week let every one of you lay by him in store, as God hath prospered him, that there be no gatherings when I come.

Having written a wonderful chapter on the resurrection—I Corinthians 15—so full of assurance and hope for every believer, Paul said, "Now concerning the collection: on the first day of the week let every one of you lay by him in store as God hath prospered him" (I Corinthians 16:1-2).

The death and resurrection of Christ were the end of the Law and the beginning of the life of grace, by which the righteousness of the Law would be fulfilled in us, including the law of proportionate giving. What before was duty, is now joy.

As those who share in the benefits of His resurrection, let us joyfully worship the Lord with our systematic, proportionate giving.

PRAYER: We thank You, Father, that You spared not Your own Son, but delivered Him up for us all, and then raised Him from the dead that we might have a living hope. Now we would show our gratitude and our joy by our offerings, presented in His name. Amen.

I CORINTHIANS 16:2
(Easter)

Upon the first day of the week let every one of you lay by him in store, as God hath prospered him, that there be no gatherings when I come.

If the salvation of which Easter speaks is worth having, it is worth sharing; and this is why we give—that others, here and abroad, may have God's salvation.

The special joy of this day is manifest in the special preparations for the day, the new clothes, a special meal, candy for the children. And how fitting to manifest it by a special gift to the Lord, to carry on the work He began that first Easter.

It was following his great chapter on the resurrection that Paul wrote, "On the first day of the week let every one of you set aside his [giving] money in the proportion that God has prospered him."

Let us worship the risen Christ with our systematic, proportionate gifts today, and every first day of the week.

PRAYER: Heavenly Father, thank You for Jesus, for His death and resurrection, and all the blessings that come to us because of it. May we, by our giving, keep that message going out, with confidence that You will supply our need. May salvation come to some because of the gifts we bring today in the name of our risen Lord and Savior. Amen.

Upon the first day of the week let every one of you lay by him in store, as God hath prospered him, that there be no gatherings when I come.

God's plan for the giving of His people is expressed in I Corinthians 16:2: "On the first day of the week let every one of you lay by him in store, as God hath prospered him." The fact that we are not under law but under grace does not release us from the responsibility of giving. Grace requires it too.

Neither do circumstances excuse us. Giving is in proportion, whether we have much or little.

Let us all give as God has prospered us as we worship the Lord.

PRAYER: Heavenly Father, as those living under grace and enjoying all the blessings of grace as we do, may we seek no excuse to spend all we have on ourselves, but fulfill Your desire for us by giving in the measure You have blessed us. May our gifts bring Your grace to others as we offer them through Jesus Christ, our Lord. Amen.

I CORINTHIANS 16:2

Upon the first day of the week let every one of you lay by him in store, as God hath prospered him, that there be no gatherings when I come.

"Upon the first day of the week let every one of you lay by him in store, as God hath prospered him."

The first day of each week comes along as a gracious reminder that God has supplied all of our needs during the past week, and that He will do the same for the coming week. He invites us to count our blessings, to name them one by one, and then give to the Lord of the first fruits of our increase.

Let us worship the Lord with our tithes and offerings in response to His goodness.

PRAYER: Heavenly Father, thank You for Your awareness of our needs, Your concern for our needs, and Your supply of our needs. Help us to be aware of the needs of others, to be concerned and to give that they too may be supplied. In Jesus' name. Amen.

Upon the first day of the week let every one of you lay by him in store, as God hath prospered him, that there be no gatherings when I come.

"On the first day of the week let every one of you lay by him in store, as God hath prospered him."

The phrase "lay by him in store," or "set aside," suggests that we should always have a giving fund, a sharing fund, from which to respond to needs brought to our attention: both the needs of the Lord's work for man's spiritual good and the material needs of our fellowman.

A woman who sends a gift each year for the work of a certain organization uses a check on which is printed "Christian work fund." You see, she puts all of her sharing money in a special checking account, as suggested by this verse. This keeps her from spending it on herself and makes it always available for others.

It is out of such a sharing fund that we worship the Lord with our systematic, proportionate gifts.

PRAYER: Heavenly Father, may our thought, whenever we receive anything, be first for others—to set aside something to share with those who have less before we begin to indulge ourselves. It is this attitude that prompts our giving to You this morning. Bless others as we have been blessed, we pray in Jesus' name. Amen.

I CORINTHIANS 16:2

Upon the first day of the week let every one of you lay by him in store, as God hath prospered him, that there be no gatherings when I come.

"On the first day of the week let every one of you lay by him in store, as God hath prospered him."

The phrase "as God hath prospered" suggests proportionate giving; like the tithe, but not a fixed proportion like the tithe, for we are not under law but under grace.

Just as the idea of one day in seven for worship is carried out in the New Testament, not on Saturday as required by the Law, but on Sunday as prompted by love, just so the idea of proportionate or percentage giving is taught in the New Testament, but without indicating the percentage, which is set not by law, but by love.

Indeed, we only worship the Lord with our proportionate gifts as they are prompted by love.

PRAYER: Heavenly Father, let us not sin in selfishness because grace abounds. Help us to abound in good works because grace has abounded in our lives. Help us abound in the good work of giving from an abounding love as we present our offerings through Jesus, our Lord. Amen.

I CORINTHIANS 16:2

Upon the first day of the week let every one of you lay by him in store, as God hath prospered him, that there be no gatherings when I come.

"On the first day of the week let every one of you lay by him in store, as God has prospered him."

Note the phrase "as God has prospered him." Our giving is to be more than a gift. It is to be a reflection of God's material blessing on us. It is to testify of God's goodness to us.

As we worship God by giving, let us be sure we worthily reflect how God has prospered us.

PRAYER: Heavenly Father, forgive us for feeling we might be doing You a favor with our offerings. May we see them, rather, as a reflection and demonstration of Your favor toward us—a witness to the world through the works of our church that you provide for our life on earth as well as in heaven. We offer our gifts through Jesus Christ, in whose name we pray. Amen.

I CORINTHIANS 16:2

Upon the first day of the week let every one of you lay by him in store, as God hath prospered him, that there be no gatherings when I come.

"On the first day of the week let every one of you lay by him in store, as God hath prospered him."

What is your TLC quotient? Proportionate, or percentage, giving reflects:

Our Trust in God—we believe His promise that He will supply our need.

Our Love and dedication to Him—we want to honor Him in this way.

Our Concern for others—with the mind of Christ we are willing to sacrifice for their good.

What does your giving reveal about your TLC quotient?

Let us think about this as we worship the Lord with that which we have laid by for giving.

PRAYER: Heavenly Father, we would be strong in our trust, deep in our love, wide in our concern. May our giving reflect growth in these areas. Multiply our gifts in human lives and the work of Your kingdom. We offer them through Christ. Amen.

I CORINTHIANS 16:2
(Tax Time)

Upon the first day of the week let every one of you lay by him in store, as God hath prospered him, that there be no gatherings when I come.

The graduated income tax recognizes that it's not how much you pay, but how much you have left that determines what your tax should be. But long before this tax table was devised God established such a principle in His plan for the giving of His people. First Corinthians 16:2, reads "On the first day of the week let every one of you lay by him in store, as God hath prospered him."

"As God hath prospered him"—that is, not only an increasing *amount*, as a set percentage of increasing income would indicate, but an increasing *percentage* as well.

Whereas the graduated tax is compelled by law, graduated giving is motivated by love and gratitude and the grace of giving.

Let us give as God has prospered us as we worship Him with our systematic, proportionate offerings.

PRAYER: Heavenly Father, may it be in our hearts to learn Your ways in life, including Your ways in giving. How can we do less than give You our best, after all You've done for us! Here is what our love and gratitude have prompted us to give today, through Jesus, our Lord. Amen.

I CORINTHIANS 16:2
(Father's Day)

Upon the first day of the week let every one of you lay by him in store, as God hath prospered him, that there be no gatherings when I come.

Since fathers, down through the ages, have usually been the breadwinners, it is obvious that instructions in the Bible about stewardship—about giving, about tithing—are directed primarily to them.

The teaching of the Old Testament is summed up in one brief statement in the New Testament—I Corinthians 16:2—which reads, "On the first day of the week let every one of you lay by him in store, as God hath prospered him."

As you fathers practice systematic, proportionate giving, you will discover that it is an important key to the solution of all your financial problems, and a key to your family's prosperity.

Let us all practice this as we now worship the Lord with our stewardship of money.

PRAYER: *Heavenly Father, thank You for the instructions for living found in Your Word, covering all phases of life. May we take them seriously, and practice them. Help the young fathers here to dare to trust You and Your Word in their financial affairs, and the older ones to testify to Your faithfulness. Receive and use that which we offer today through Jesus Christ, our Lord. Amen.*

I CORINTHIANS 16:2
(Fathers Day)

Upon the first day of the week let every one of you lay by him in store, as God hath prospered him, that there be no gatherings when I come.

"On the first day of the week let every one of you lay by him in store, as God hath prospered him."

This instruction for systematic, proportionate giving is basically for fathers. They are the head of the house and as such determine the principles and program of the family, including its stewardship. They are the ones, primarily, who earn the living and determine the budget. They are the ones who set an example for the children—the Christians of the next generation—to follow.

Let the Christian fathers of this church obey this Scripture as we worship the Lord with our systematic, proportionate giving.

PRAYER: Heavenly Father, may our giving express our own gratitude and sense of responsibility, and may it also be an example to our children that they may learn the grace of giving. Take these offerings we make today and make other families here and abroad richer through them, we pray in Jesus' name. Amen.

I CORINTHIANS 16:2
(For Graduates)

Upon the first day of the week let every one of you lay by him in store, as God hath prospered him, that there be no gatherings when I come.

MALACHI 3:10

Bring ye all the tithes into the storehouse, that there may be meat in mine house, and prove me now herewith, saith the Lord of hosts, if I will not open you the windows of heaven, and pour you out a blessing, that there shall not be room enough to receive it.

A word to you graduates about giving:

You are entering a new phase of life, where you will be earning your own money and paying your own way. This is the time to begin to learn the grace of giving, and to start practicing systematic, proportionate giving; that is, giving God a definite percentage of all your income. Even if you are going on to college, now is the time to begin this practice. It is the only guarantee of your own prosperity—and it is good stewardship.

All of God's promises to supply your need, as a student or as a homemaker, or whatever your occupation, are related to your giving to supply the needs of others, especially their spiritual needs. This is true of every promise in the Bible.

God's command to you is found in I Corinthians 16:2: "On the first day of the week let every one of you lay by him in store, as God hath prospered him."

God's promise to you is recorded in Malachi 3:10: "Bring all the tithes into the storehouse and prove me now herewith, saith the Lord, if I will not open for you the windows of heaven, and pour out for you a blessing, that there shall not be room enough to receive it."

I commend to you the Christian practice of systematic, proportionate giving, and urge you to begin it today.

Let us all practice it as we worship the Lord with our tithes and offerings.

PRAYER: *Heavenly Father, thank You for these Christian young people now beginning to take places of responsibility in our society. May they early learn the grace of giving, and that it is more blessed to give than to receive. Put a regard for the needs of others in their hearts; give them the mind of Christ, and help them to have the thrill of discovering that keeping all for self is to become poorer, while sharing with others is to become richer. Help us older ones to be a good example to them. Increase the worth of our offerings today in human lives. In Jesus' name. Amen.*

I CORINTHIANS 16:2
(Year's End)

Upon the first day of the week let every one of you lay by him in store, as God hath prospered him, that there be no gatherings when I come.

As the end of the year approaches, it is not uncommon for people to check to see if they are "up-to-date" in their giving; that is, have they given week by week and not fallen behind.

But there is another aspect of being up-to-date in giving: if our giving does not increase as our income increases we are not up-to-date in our giving. If we are giving the same now as we gave a few years ago, we are failing to recognize that things now cost more in the Lord's work, too.

The only way to be up-to-date in giving is by systematic, proportionate giving, giving a percentage *of* our income that keeps pace *with* our income.

"On the first day of the week let every one of you lay by him in store, as God hath prospered him" (I Corinthians 16:2).

Let us worship the Lord with up-to-date giving.

PRAYER: Heavenly Father, things are costing more now, even for us, but You are supplying our need, and we would not rob You by withholding more than is right. Teach us the grace of proportionate giving, and use what we bring for enduring works, through Jesus Christ, our Lord. Amen.

I CORINTHIANS 16:2
(New Year's Day)

Upon the first day of the week let every one of you lay by him in store, as God hath prospered him, that there be no gatherings when I come.

"On the first day of the week let every one of you lay by him in store, as God hath prospered him."

At this beginning of a new year it is well to remind ourselves that God's program for faithful stewardship is systematic, proportionate giving.

Start it now, make it a practice, and at year's end more will have been given, more good will have been done, more joy will be in your heart, more treasure will be laid up in heaven, and there will be no sense of failure.

With a proper proportion, according to our income, let us worship the Lord with our tithes and offerings.

PRAYER: Heavenly Father, just as we make provision in our budget for the other obligations and desires of the year, we would make provision for our giving. Help us to see our offerings, not as something going from us, only, but going to some worthy work, and to rejoice in the good it will do. In Jesus' name. Amen.

Upon the first day of the week let every one of you lay by him in store, as God hath prospered him, that there be no gatherings when I come.

A paraphrase of I Corinthians 16:2 says, "Let every one of you lay aside his giving money in the proportion that God has prospered him, that there be no last minute offering." That is, to borrow an old phrase, "charity begins at home," not when the offering plate is passed.

Those who wait till the time of the offering to see what they have in their purse and to decide what they will give, will never be good stewards and will never make the work of God go forward.

What we give in church on Sunday should be planned at home ahead of time. Then we can determine the proportion or percentage we will give; we can think about the causes to which we will give it; we can pray for guidance, and as a consequence we will give it gladly and there will be a dedication of self and substance that God can bless.

Let us give as we have planned as we worship the Lord with our giving money.

PRAYER: *Heavenly Father, with the same forethought and care with which we make our other expenditures, may we give to Thee week by week. Thank You for supplying our needs this week. From that supply we bring this offering this morning, and present it through the merit of our Savior, Jesus Christ. Amen.*

I CORINTHIANS 16:2

Upon the first day of the week let every one of you lay by him in store, as God hath prospered him, that there be no gatherings when I come.

"On the first day of the week let every one of you lay by him in store, as God hath prospered him."

Systematic, proportionate giving testifies to our belief that God is the Lord of our lives and of all that we have; not just of our income, but of all our possessions and talents and time.

Some think their service excuses them from giving; others think their giving excuses them from serving. Neither is true.

Our Christian stewardship requires that we seek the Lord's guidance in all our living, and seek to honor Him with our substance, our abilities, our opportunities, and our time.

"To whom much is given, of him much will be required," said Jesus in Luke 12:48. Who of us can say we have not been given much?

Let us acknowledge the Lordship of Christ in the way we worship Him with our tithes and offerings.

PRAYER: Heavenly Father, help us to see our offering today not as some generous gesture on our part, but as good stewardship to Thee, the Lord of our lives. In Jesus' name. Amen.

I CORINTHIANS 16:2

Upon the first day of the week let every one of you lay by him in store as God hath prospered him, that there be no gatherings when I come.

"On the first day of the week let every one of you lay by him in store, as God hath prospered him."

Systematic and proportionate giving, regularly giving a definite percentage of our income to the Lord, is God's plan for the support of His work.

I do not know your personal financial situation, but I commend you for the faith and courage you have shown in assuming responsibility for the local work, the building program, and the worldwide ministry of this church.

These goals and obligations will be met as we all practice systematic and proportionate giving. Many of us have also found that this is the key to blessing in our own lives and homes.

Let us consider this as we worship the Lord with that which we have laid aside for this purpose.

PRAYER: Heavenly Father, thank You for the privilege of being a part of Your church and having a part in Your work. We are not worthy to give, but we present these offerings through Jesus Christ, our Lord. Amen.

Upon the first day of the week let every one of you lay by him in store, as God hath prospered him, that there be no gatherings when I come.

"On the first day of the week let every one of you lay by him in store, as God hath prospered him."

One of the reasons why giving sometimes irritates us is that we are prone to think in terms of what the *church needs*, instead of what the *Lord wants*. There is no end of need in the world, nor of the effort of the church to witness to the world. Not one of us can meet it all. But we will do a lot, and will find real joy in doing it, if we just make it our concern, as we read our Bible and pray, to discover what the Lord wants us to give.

Systematic, proportionate giving is the basic plan of God, to be worked out in each individual Christian life, not on the compulsion of law, but by the constraint of love.

On this basis let us worship the Lord as God has prospered us.

PRAYER: Heavenly Father, may we ever be aware of the need of others and desire to help. But may our giving be influenced by what You want us to give, as You have revealed it in Your Word. May our offerings today be measured by what You have given us. In Jesus' name. Amen.

I CORINTHIANS 16:2

Upon the first day of the week let every one of you lay by him in store, as God hath prospered him, that there be no gatherings when I come.

"On the first day of the week let every one of you lay by him in store, as God hath prospered him."

God's plan is to supply our need and have us give a tithe—that is, 10 percent—back to him. And we have been living well, haven't we!

Now suppose God reversed this and said: "You give, and I will multiply your gift by ten and give it back to you for your needs." Could you live on it? Would you be living as well?

The Lord promises to prosper us *as we give*. Maybe *that* is our problem.

Let us worship the Lord with our tithes and offerings.

PRAYER: Heavenly Father, we are so glad You are patient with us, and gracious to us, and that You do supply our needs. Now may we cheerfully respond with our systematic, proportionate giving as You have prospered us. Make these offerings a blessing in the lives of other people. In Jesus' name. Amen.

Upon the first day of the week let every one of you lay by him in store, as God hath prospered him, that there be no gatherings when I come.

"On the first day of the week let every one of you lay by him in store, as God hath prospered him."

It is an established principle that our giving is to be according to our earnings. What do you suppose would happen if, on the other hand, God were to determine our earnings according to our giving? Would we be richer, or poorer? This is, in fact, another of His established principles.

Let us worship the Lord with our systematic, proportionate giving.

PRAYER: Heavenly Father, it is just like You to give first and ask second, and to ask us to give in the measure You have given to us. With reverence for You and gratitude for Your gifts, we lay our offerings before You today for Your use in the lives of people, through Jesus Christ, our Lord. Amen.

Upon the first day of the week let every one of you lay by him in store, as God hath prospered him, that there be no gatherings when I come.

"On the first day of the week let every one of you lay by him in store, as God hath prospered him."

Some look on giving as an obligation which they would like to escape.

Some consider it a favor they are doing.

Christians consider it a privilege—to give to God and help people; an investment—with present returns in the lives of people, and eternal returns in the presence of Christ; and a stewardship—a responsible use of all that is given to them, of which they will be glad to give account at the judgment seat of Christ.

Let us think about this matter as we worship the Lord with our systematic, proportionate giving.

PRAYER: Heavenly Father, may we never give grudgingly or of necessity, not after You have done so much for us and are supplying our need every day. May we count our giving a privilege, and do it in good stewardship. Here is our investment for today. Add Your blessing to it as we offer it through Jesus Christ, our Lord. Amen.

I CORINTHIANS 16:2

Upon the first day of the week let every one of you lay by him in store, as God hath prospered him, that there be no gatherings when I come.

Overall dedication of one's life to Christ means little unless it is followed by specific dedication in particular areas.

In the area of possessions, the best way to show our dedication is to give God a definite percentage of all of our income. The size of the percentage, at first, is not as important as the definiteness of it. And true dedication is demonstrated in one's openness to increase the percentage as God directs and as the standard of living improves.

In a spirit of true dedication, on this first day of the week, let us worship the Lord as He has prospered us.

PRAYER: Heavenly Father, we consider ourselves dedicated to You. Help us express our dedication in specific ways. May our giving today, and every week, reveal a true dedication of all of our resources to our Lord, who is worthy because He has redeemed us by His blood. And use these gifts to help other lives, we pray in Jesus' name. Amen.

I CORINTHIANS 16:2

Upon the first day of the week let every one of you lay by him in store, as God hath prospered him, that there be no gatherings when I come.

The widow seemed, to onlookers, to be giving only a part; Jesus knew she was giving all. Ananias and Sapphira seemed to be giving all; God knew they were giving only a part. The widow gained immortal fame. Ananias and Sapphira gained immortal shame. God judges our giving not by the amount but by the proportion.

On this first day of the week, let us worship the Lord with that which we have set aside for giving as God has prospered us.

PRAYER: Heavenly Father, we do not give to gain man's approval, but to gain Yours, not in fear but in love. And so we count it a privilege to give joyously and proportionately this morning. May others be enriched thereby, through Jesus, in whose name we offer these gifts. Amen.

I CORINTHIANS 16:2

Upon the first day of the week let every one of you lay by him in store, as God hath prospered him, that there be no gatherings when I come.

"On the first day of the week let every one of you lay by him in store [set aside his giving] as God hath prospered him."

Note the phrase "as God hath prospered him." That is, giving is not to be in proportion to the needs of the church or the world, but in proportion to our income. Then God will direct in the use of it for the needs at home and abroad.

We do not learn about the needs and then decide how much we can give; rather, we decide to give, and God directs where.

Let us give today, not in response to needs, but in response to the love that has blessed us.

PRAYER: Heavenly Father, give us a right slant on our giving. May we give to You and not to the church, and may we give before we are aware of needs, because we love You and are grateful. Then guide Your church in the right use of these gifts, offered through Jesus Christ, our Lord. Amen.

II CORINTHIANS 4:3

But if our gospel be hid, it is hid to them that are lost.

"If our gospel be hid it is hid to them that are lost."

If we withhold more of the substance God has given us than we should, we withhold the gospel from people who have never heard it—people who are without God and without hope unless we send the gospel to them.

Half the world has never heard the gospel; many more have not heard it sufficiently to be saved. Dare we deprive them of the opportunity of eternal life when God has so freely provided it for us?

For their sakes let us worship the Lord with our systematic, proportionate giving.

PRAYER: Heavenly Father, thank You for the gospel. Thank You for those who gave that we might hear. Help us to give in such a measure that no one will be deprived of the opportunity of hearing and believing in our Lord Jesus Christ, through whom we make these offerings. Amen.

II CORINTHIANS 5:9

Wherefore we labour, that, whether present or absent, we may be accepted of him.

Second Corinthians 5:9 suggests a good motto for Christians, one that covers one's life in its entirety: "We make it our aim to please Him."

We make this our aim because we love Him who first loved us. Thus the extent of our aim is the whole of our life, including our giving—giving not grudgingly, but cheerfully and generously. When, before the service, we prepare our offering, it is good to ask, "Is this pleasing to Him?" If we are satisfied that it is, then we will be able to truly worship the Lord with our tithes and offerings.

PRAYER: Heavenly Father, we do love You; we do want to please You in all things; we want our giving to be pleasing in Your sight—not so much that You will approve what we give as that we will give what You can approve. In this spirit we bring our offerings this morning and offer them to You, not because we are worthy to, but through Jesus Christ, our Lord. Amen.

Moreover, brethren, we do you to wit of the grace of God bestowed on the churches of Macedonia; how that in a great trial of affliction the abundance of their joy and their deep poverty abounded unto the riches of their liberality.

How can you tell when the grace of God is working in a person's life? By the way they give, for there is nothing closer to ourselves than our substance.

Second Corinthians 8:1 says, "We do you to wit [that is, we want you to know] of the grace of God bestowed on the churches of Macedonia." How will we know? "In a great trial of affliction the abundance of their joy and their deep poverty abounded unto the riches of their liberality." *That's* some equation! a supernatural one: it's the grace of God. Deep poverty plus abundant joy equals liberality.

Few of us have known anything of deep poverty, but if the joy of His grace is working in our lives it will make us liberal as we worship the Lord with our systematic, proportionate giving.

PRAYER: Heavenly Father, we thank You for all we have, materially and spiritually. May it be our joy this morning to be liberal in our giving for the needs of others. Receive and bless Your gifts, offered in the merit of our Savior. Amen.

II CORINTHIANS 8:1-2

Moreover, brethren, we do you to wit of the grace of God bestowed on the churches of Macedonia; how that in a great trial of affliction the abundance of their joy and their deep poverty abounded unto the riches of their liberality.

In II Corinthians 8:1 and 2 Paul says, "I call your attention to the manifestation of God's grace in the churches of Macedonia, how that in a great trial of affliction they have been so joyful that from the depths of their poverty they have shown themselves very generous."

Spirituality is not only measured in terms of the prayer life, Bible knowledge, and Christian service—distinctions reserved, perhaps, for the few. It is also measured in the use of our money, which we all have, and in which we can all be spiritual.

As an exercise in spirituality and as a manifestation of God's grace, let us worship the Lord with our generous giving.

PRAYER: Heavenly Father, may our spirituality be more than pious emotions; may it be very practical, showing itself in our dealings with other people, and for other people. By Your grace we present our offerings this morning through the merit of our Lord, Jesus Christ. Amen.

II CORINTHIANS 8:1-2

Moreover, brethren, we do you to wit of the grace of God bestowed on the churches of Macedonia; how that in a great trial of affliction the abundance of their joy and their deep poverty abounded unto the riches of their liberality.

Concerning the Macedonian Christians, Paul said, "In a great trial of affliction the abundance of their joy and their deep poverty abounded unto the riches of their liberality" (II Corinthians 8:2).

There is an algebraic equation in giving: $A = C/R$.

The Amount we give equals our Commitment in relation to our Resources. If we are committed to the principle of systematic, proportionate giving because we want to please and honor the Lord, we will always find a way to give liberally, with joy and without griping.

May we know this grace of giving and demonstrate it as we worship the Lord out of the abundance of our joy.

PRAYER: Heavenly Father, thank You for making it possible for us to give, and for being willing to receive our gifts. Search our hearts to know our motive as we give, and look at our accounts to see if we have given properly. Then add Your blessing to the gifts and Your guidance to their use, we pray in Jesus' name. Amen.

II CORINTHIANS 8:5

And this they did, not as we hoped, but first gave their own selves to the Lord, and unto us by the will of God.

The Macedonian Christians first gave their own selves to the Lord, and then, as the grace of God worked in them, they gave liberally of their substance. It is not hard to give our substance when we have given ourselves to Him. And our substance doesn't mean much to Him until we give ourselves.

Let us reckon both ourselves and our substance His as we worship Him with our systematic, proportionate giving.

PRAYER: Lord Jesus, You are worthy to receive both ourselves and our substance, for You have redeemed us to God by Your blood. Through Your merit we now present our offerings. Make them a blessing to other lives. Amen.

II CORINTHIANS 8:5

And this they did, not as we hoped, but first gave their own selves to the Lord, and unto us by the will of God.

According to II Corinthians 8:5, the Macedonian Christians first gave themselves to the Lord, and then besought Paul, with much entreaty, that he would receive their gift. Literally "they begged of him the favour of sharing in his ministry" (Weymouth).

The needs of the church for its ministry become a Christian's concern when giving becomes an act of worship. We never want anyone to give because we have needs; we do want every Christian to give to the Lord because they love Him and share His concern for others.

Let the outward gift be an expression of an inward devotion as we worship the Lord with our systematic, proportionate gifts this morning.

PRAYER: Heavenly Father, we do not give out of necessity, but out of love; not in response to a plea, but we initiate our giving because we are dedicated to You and Your work in the world. With our offerings today we are saying we want to be a part of the ministry! Accept the offerings of our hearts and our hands as we present them through Jesus Christ, our Lord. Amen.

II CORINTHIANS 8:7

Therefore, as ye abound in every thing, in faith, and utterance, and knowledge, and in all diligence, and in your love to us, see that ye abound in this grace also.

"As you abound in every sort of spiritual quality—in faith, in witnessing, in knowledge [of the Bible], in zeal and loyalty, and in love—see that you abound in the grace of giving also."

Some would rather give than serve; some would rather serve than give. The Bible teaches that the grace of God must be allowed to work in us so that everything that is precious to us—our time, our talents, and our tithes—is devoted to the Lord, and that in everything we give not our bit but our best.

May our substance be devoted to Him as we worship Him in the grace of giving.

PRAYER: Heavenly Father, we would not dictate how we will serve You. Rather, may we respond to the leading of Your Holy Spirit as He directs our out-working of Your grace in our lives. We trust that our gifts today reflect this spirit as we offer them through Jesus Christ, our Lord. Amen.

Therefore, as ye abound in every thing, in faith, and utterance, and knowledge, and in all diligence, and in your love to us, see that ye abound in this grace also.

"See that you abound in the grace of giving."

In the Old Testament, the law of the tithe was the minimum starting point for giving; it meant proportionate and systematic giving and it was to be from the first part of the income.

In the New Testament, we are not under the Law, but systematic, proportionate giving is prescribed, and tithing is a good starting point. Further, we are admonished to put God first.

Those who have tried this have found it to be a greater blessing than anything the Israelites ever knew. They would not go back to haphazard giving.

Let us abound in the grace of giving as we worship the Lord with our proportionate gifts.

PRAYER: Heavenly Father, may Your grace teach us to give not the least, but the most; that, as those who have life in Christ, we might fulfill all the righteousness of the Law. Help our church to invest our offerings wisely and profitably in the work of the gospel, we pray in Jesus' name. Amen.

II CORINTHIANS 8:7

Therefore, as ye abound in every thing, in faith, and utterance, and knowledge, and in all diligence, and in your love to us, see that ye abound in this grace also.

"As you abound in every sort of spiritual quality, see that you abound in the grace of giving also."

Many of us are anxious to grow in grace in the areas of victory over sin and in Christlikeness. We need also to be concerned about growing in the grace of giving.

If we regularly observe what the Scriptures teach about this, and regularly pray about it, we will abound in this grace also, and be glad.

Let God see that we abound in this grace as we worship Him with our systematic, proportionate giving.

PRAYER: Heavenly Father, help us to be satisfied with nothing less than pleasing You in all things, in all areas of our lives. May we strive to please You in the area of giving, and may our offering today indicate to You that we are, indeed, growing in this grace, through Jesus Christ, our Lord. Amen.

Therefore, as ye abound in every thing, in faith, and utterance, and knowledge, and in all diligence, and in your love to us, see that ye abound in this grace also.

Dr. Alan Redpath, former pastor of Moody Church in Chicago, tells a most interesting story in his book *The Royal Route to Heaven*.

A certain Christian once said to a friend, "Our church costs too much. They are always asking for money." The friend replied thus, "Some time ago a little boy was born into our home. He cost a lot from the very beginning. He had a big appetite, he needed clothes, medicine, toys, even a puppy. Then he went to school and that cost a lot more. Later he went to college; then he began dating and that cost a small fortune! But in his senior year of college he was stricken ill and died. Since his funeral he hasn't cost me a penny. Now, which situation do you think I would rather have?"

After a pause he continued, "As long as a church lives it will cost money. When it dies for want of support, it won't cost anything. A living church has the most vital message for the world today. I am going to give and pray with everything I have to keep my church alive."

(Published by Fleming H. Revell Co. and used by permission.)

"As you abound in other aspects of your Christian life, see that you abound in the grace of giving also," as we worship the Lord with our systematic, proportionate giving.

PRAYER: *Heavenly Father, thank You for Your church, which has prevailed against all the forces of evil through the centuries, and has ministered to us meaningfully in our lifetime. We count it a pleasure to help it continue a dynamic program for the temporal and eternal blessing of others, and so bring our offerings today through our Lord, Jesus Christ. Amen.*

Therefore, as ye abound in every thing, in faith, and utterance, and knowledge, and in all diligence, and in your love to us, see that ye abound in this grace also.

In II Corinthians 8:7 Paul says, "See that ye abound in the grace of giving."

On the whole, giving a percentage of our income is better than giving a fixed amount. But even the percentage need not be fixed. At whatever percentage we start, let us be open to increase it as God proves Himself faithful in supplying our needs.

If, when we are young and our income or our faith is small, we start at a certain percentage, then as increases come, we might consider not only a percentage of the larger income, but also increasing the percentage. In this way we will begin to abound in the grace of giving.

In gratitude and love, let us manifest that we are abounding in this grace as we worship our Lord with our proportionate giving.

PRAYER: Heavenly Father, You have abounded toward us in grace. We want to abound toward You in giving. Help us to overcome selfishness and fear, and to dare to step out into larger spheres of giving. This morning we give in the measure of our faith and love. Direct this church as it uses these funds, we pray through Jesus Christ, our Lord. Amen.

II CORINTHIANS 8:7-9

Therefore, as ye abound in every thing, in faith, and utterance, and knowledge, and in all diligence, and in your love to us, see that ye abound in this grace also. I speak not by commandment, but by occasion of the forwardness of others, and to prove the sincerity of your love. For ye know the grace of our Lord Jesus Christ, that, though he was rich, yet for your sakes he became poor, that ye through his poverty might be rich.

In II Corinthians 8:7-8 Paul informs the Corinthian Christians that "abounding in the grace of giving proves the sincerity of your love" (v. 9, optional).

You see, giving is not to *buy* grace, but is a *response to* grace. And since grace is given constantly and according to our need, our giving should not be haphazard, but systematic—each payday; and proportionate—that is, tithing a definite percentage of all we receive.

So with sincere love let us worship the Lord with our systematic, proportionate giving, not in obedience to the Law, but in response to grace.

PRAYER: Heavenly Father, thank You for Your grace, Your response to our need. Move our hearts to respond to the needs of others, spiritual and material needs, by sharing what we have because of our gratitude for Your grace. Since You know our hearts, You know what our offerings are saying this morning. We want them to say, "I love You." In Jesus' name. Amen.

II CORINTHIANS 8:8

I speak not by commandment, but by occasion of the forwardness of others, and to prove the sincerity of your love.

In II Corinthians 8:8 we read, "Giving proves the sincerity of our love."

It is easy to sing, "O how I love Jesus," but the real measure of our love is demonstrated by how much of our substance we give to Him. We may intend to do a lot when we are emotionally moved by the needs of others, but our concern is measured by our giving.

Let God see that our love is sincere as we worship Him now with our systematic, proportionate giving.

PRAYER: Heavenly Father, we do love You. We say we do. And we do. Yet, perhaps You have not seen the proof of it in our giving. This morning we want to show You that we love You, so we present these offerings we have prepared. In the name of Your Unspeakable Gift. Amen.

II CORINTHIANS 8:9
(Christmas)

For we know the grace of our Lord Jesus Christ, that, though he was rich, yet for your sakes he became poor, that ye through his poverty might be rich.

The story of Christmas is summed up in these words, "You know the grace of our Lord Jesus Christ, that though he was rich, yet for our sakes he became poor, that we through his poverty might be rich."

When offered a low-paying job in Christian service, a Christian recently said, "I am not planning poverty." Jesus *did*—He voluntarily impoverished Himself that others might be rich in eternal things.

We have that same opportunity, at Christmas and all the year, to give what we might spend on ourselves in order that others might hear the gospel and be saved.

Let us enter into the Christmas spirit as we worship the Lord with our systematic, proportionate gifts.

PRAYER: Thank You, Lord Jesus, that You were willing to lay aside your heavenly glory in order that we might be with You in glory. Help us to have a mind for others, and to give for their enrichment. Receive and use these gifts, offered in Thy name. Amen.

II CORINTHIANS 8:9

For ye know the grace of our Lord Jesus Christ, that, though he was rich, yet for your sakes he became poor, that ye through his poverty might be rich.

To give, we must do without something. But what is it we do without? Seldom is it anything we really need; usually it is some passing, paltry bauble. And what is the result of doing without it? Others have the precious Word of life. Isn't this better?

"Ye know the grace of our Lord Jesus Christ, that, though he was rich, yet for our sakes he became poor, that we through his poverty might be rich."

For the enrichment of others, at our expense, let us worship the Lord with our systematic, proportionate giving.

PRAYER: Heavenly Father, as we remember how low our Lord stooped and from what heights, that our lives might be rich, we would reduce our spending in order to give, that others might be rich in the knowledge of Christ. To this end bless these offerings, we pray in His name. Amen.

II CORINTHIANS 8:9

For ye know the grace of our Lord Jesus Christ, that, though he was rich, yet for your sakes he became poor, that ye through his poverty might be rich.

"You know the grace of our Lord Jesus Christ, that, though he was rich, yet for our sakes he became poor, that we through his poverty might be rich."

This example of our Lord Jesus prescibes the motive for our giving; we should give of our material things to enrich others in spiritual and eternal things. It is a worthy purpose. The more faithfully we follow His example, the more good we will do and the happier we will be.

Let this be our motive as we worship the Lord with our systematic, proportionate giving.

PRAYER: Heavenly Father, we acknowledge that our lives are richer because our Savior became poorer. May these offerings reflect the mind of Christ, a mind attuned to the needs of others, as we present them to You through Him. Amen.

II CORINTHIANS 8:10-11
(Year's End)

And herein I give my advice: for this is expedient for you, who have begun before, not only to do, but also to be forward a year ago. Now therefore perform the doing of it; that as there was a readiness to will, so there may be a perfomance also out of that which ye have.

Speaking of Christians making a faith-promise for giving, in II Corinthians 8:10-11 Paul says, "You began a year ago, not only to give, but to desire or purpose to give. Now, therefore, fulfill your purpose by your giving; that as you then showed a readiness to give, so now let your giving correspond to your readiness, in proportion to your means."

As the end of the year approached I checked to see if I had given as much as I intended to; and at the same time, as the new year approaches I am considering what my faith-promise will be for the coming year.

This will guide our family as we readily worship the Lord with our systematic, proportionate giving.

PRAYER: Heavenly Father, as we make covenants with the merchants and plan our finances accordingly, may we not hesitate to make a covenant with You and plan our giving accordingly. You are worthy of this honor as we give to You now through Jesus Christ, our Lord. Amen.

II CORINTHIANS 8:12

For if there be first a willing mind, it is accepted according to that a man hath, and not according to that he hath not.

"If there be first a willing mind, it is accepted according to what a man has, and not according to what he has not."

According to a modern translation, "It's not what you'd do with a million, if riches should ever be your lot; but what are you doing now with the dollar and a quarter you've got?"

God doesn't expect us to give what we don't have, but He does promise to bless those who give in proportion to what they do have. This is the principle of tithing. First we relinquish in our mind and heart our claim to all our substance; then God recognizes not the amount we give but the proportion. Let us willingly worship Him with a proper proportion of what we have.

PRAYER: Heavenly Father, give us willing minds to share with You the substance You have given us, that You may further meet the needs of others, especially for the gospel. We trust that our giving this morning is according to what we have, and so is acceptable in Your sight, through Jesus Christ, our Lord. Amen.

For if there be first a willing mind, it is accepted according to that a man hath, and not according to that he hath not.

"If there be first a willing mind, it is accepted according to what a man has, and not according to what he doesn't have."

God is not as concerned with *how much* we give as with *how* we give. If we are willing to give, and willing to give according to His guidelines, He will be pleased with the amount.

Let it be with willing minds that we worship the Lord with a systematic proportion of what we have.

PRAYER: Heavenly Father, we are not always willing to give, but at least we are willing to be made willing. Work in our hearts so that week after week we have willing minds to share a proper proportion of our income. You know the measure of our willingness as revealed by our offerings today. Help us to grow in willingness, and guide the church in its use of the gifts we bring, through Jesus Christ, our Lord. Amen.

II CORINTHIANS 8:12

For if there be first a willing mind, it is accepted according to that a man hath, and not according to that he hath not.

II CORINTHIANS 9:8

And God is able to make all grace abound toward you; that ye, always having all sufficiency in all things, may abound to every good work.

A Christian family was hit with three major expenses at the very time their church presented a Building Fund need. They didn't see how they could contribute toward it. One of the expenses was a new well. They didn't know how deep they might have to go, but they said, "Lord, we will allot enough for that well to go to 200 feet, but if You will bring it in shallower, we will give to the Building Fund." The well came in at 37 feet, and they brought their gift that week for the Building Fund.

This reminds us of II Corinthians 8:12: "If there be first a willing mind, it is accepted according to what a man has, and not according to what he doesn't have," and II Corinthians 9:8: "God is able to make all grace abound toward you, that you, always having all sufficiency in all things, may abound to every good work."

With willing minds, let us worship the Lord according to what we have.

PRAYER: *Heavenly Father, thank You that these people wanted to give, and that You made it possible for them to give. May we want to give too. You have made it possible for us to give today, and so we bring these offerings through our Lord, Jesus Christ. Amen.*

II CORINTHIANS 8:13-14

For I mean not that other men be eased, and ye burdened: but by an equality, that now at this time your abundance may be a supply for their want, that their abundance also may be a supply for your want: that there may be equality.

Second Corinthians 8:13-14 teaches that our giving is not to make others better off and ourselves worse off, but to create an equality. God is concerned with equality.

We are all aware of some who have more than we have, but we need to consider how many have less, materially and spiritually, as we worship the Lord with our systematic, proportionate giving.

PRAYER: *Heavenly Father, thank You for all You have given us. Overcome the covetousness in our hearts that wants to get more, or to keep all we have. Help us to regularly remember those who have less, and to give to lift their burden, through Jesus Christ, our Lord. Amen.*

But by an equality, that now at this time your abundance may be a supply for their want, that their abundance also may be a supply for your want: that there may be equality.

Godless communism has as its slogan, "From each according to his ability; to each according to his need." This is but an imitation of Christianity, and many respond to it.

Yet long before communism appeared in the world the Bible said this concerning giving, " . . . that now at this time your abundance may be a supply for their want, that their abundance also may be a supply for your want, that there may be equality" (II Corinthians 8:14). People see the communist slogan as a way of getting. Christians see the Biblical statement as a way of giving.

The greatest need of all is mankind's spiritual need, and as Christians respond to the Lord's plan that need will be met.

It is to meet that need by sharing that we worship the Lord with our systematic, proportionate giving.

PRAYER: Heavenly Father, may our hearts in which You dwell respond as readily to Your plan as the natural heart does to the schemes of man. May the mind of Christ, a mind displaying concern for others, motivate us as we give today through our Lord, Jesus Christ. Amen.

II CORINTHIANS 8:15

As it is written, He that had gathered much had nothing over; and he that had gathered little had no lack.

Referring to God's daily supply of manna for the Israelites, II Corinthians 8:15 says, "He that had gathered much had nothing over; and he that had gathered little had no lack"; which means, he that was selfish or greedy and trusted in his own ideas about security did not end up with more than he needed, whereas the man who trusted God and obeyed Him in sharing did not end up with less than he needed.

This is a lesson for us to remember as we worship the Lord with our systematic, proportionate giving.

PRAYER: Heavenly Father, we are slow to learn that Your ways are better than our ways and Your thoughts than our thoughts, but we want to learn. Help us to handle our finances as those who trust and obey because we believe Your way is best. Thank You for supplying our needs and making possible our offerings today through our Lord, Jesus Christ. Amen.

Wherefore shew ye to them, and before the churches, the proof of your love, and of our boasting on your behalf.

Concerning their giving, Paul wrote to the Corinthians, "Show the proof of your love."

Our giving tells several things about us: how much we love the Lord; how much we trust God and His promises to meet our needs; how well we have learned the grace of giving; how faithful we are in our stewardship; how much we care for the work of the Lord; how much we want our church to make an impact in the world; and how well we have overcome covetousness, which is idolatry.

These things are revealed more by our giving than by our words.

Let us show the proof of our love as we worship the Lord with our systematic, proportionate giving.

PRAYER: Heavenly Father, we pray that our love for Thee may overcome our love for things and for security, and thus enable us to give liberally to meet the needs of a world lost in sin. Speak to our hearts concerning the measure of our giving. Receive our gifts as a measure of our love, offered through Jesus Christ, our Lord. Amen.

II CORINTHIANS 9:2

For I know the forwardness of your mind, for which I boast of you to them of Macedonia, that Achaia was ready a year ago; and your zeal provoked very many.

Concerning the giving of the Corinthian Christians, Paul said in II Corinthians 9:2, "Your zeal hath stimulated very many."

Some folks gauge their giving by what others give. Some, moved with zeal for God and His work, lead the way with spontaneous, generous, cheerful giving. Thank God for this kind of people in the church. They are the ones who make greater things possible.

May we be motivated by zeal and lead the way as we worship God with our systematic, proportionate giving.

PRAYER: Heavenly Father, in giving, make us leaders as we respond to Your leadership in loving giving, for You spared not your own Son, but delivered Him up for us all. With such an example, we would not follow man, but would stimulate others as we give through Your Son. Amen.

Therefore I thought it necessary to exhort the brethren, that they would go before unto you, and make up beforehand your bounty, whereof ye had notice before, that the same might be ready, as a matter of bounty, and not as of covetousness.

Speaking of the offering, Paul said to the Corinthian Christians, "Have it ready beforehand, that it might be a matter of bounty (on your part), and not a matter of covetousness (on our part); that is, that it might be what you want to give, not what the church wants to collect; might be given freely and not under pressure; might be given spontaneously and not squeezed out of you."

May we always give in this way as we worship the Lord with our bounties prepared beforehand.

PRAYER: *Heavenly Father, may our giving not be in response to the church's call, but in response to our own heart's prompting. Develop in us gratitude and love and concern. We want You to know today that our offerings are given freely, through Jesus Christ, our Lord. Amen.*

II CORINTHIANS 9:6

But this I say, He which soweth sparingly shall reap also sparingly; and he which soweth bountifully shall reap also bountifully.

We can't take our money with us, but we can send it on ahead. Second Corinthians 9:6 says, "He who soweth sparingly shall reap also sparingly; he who soweth bountifully shall reap also bountifully."

Our giving on earth determines our reward in heaven, and the greatest reward will be the joy of seeing what our giving accomplished and who it brought to heaven.

Let us have both the present need and future harvest in mind as we worship the Lord with our bountiful giving.

PRAYER: *Heavenly Father, help us to consider not only the passing joys of earth, but to earnestly consider the lasting joys of heaven: Your joy, the joy of the redeemed, as well as our own joy, and to give to increase all that joy. May our offerings today accomplish much in human lives as we present them through our Lord, Jesus Christ. Amen.*

II CORINTHIANS 9:6

But this I say, He which soweth sparingly shall reap also sparingly; and he which soweth bountifully shall reap also bountifully.

Concerning giving, II Corinthians 9:6 says, "He who sows sparingly shall reap sparingly; he who sows bountifully shall reap bountifully."

Man's wisdom frequently suggests to us that "we can't afford to give too much"; but in many ways, in many Scripture passages, God teaches that we can't afford to give too little. In giving too little, we not only rob God, but rob ourselves. In giving bountifully we increase our own blessing.

PRAYER: Heavenly Father, teach us to live and to give by Your wisdom, not by ours. May we trust Your wisdom as well as Your grace. Judge our giving this morning for its bountifulness in the light of our means, we pray in Jesus' name. Amen.

II CORINTHIANS 9:6

But this I say, He which soweth sparingly shall reap also sparingly; and he which soweth bountifully shall reap also bountifully.

Concerning giving, the Bible says, "He who soweth sparingly shall reap also sparingly; he who soweth bountifully shall reap also bountifully" (II Corinthians 9:6).

Giving has its own effect on our lives, according to laws built into the universe. Thus we rob ourselves when we rob God. But if we are generous toward God, He will be generous toward us.

Let us sow bountifully as we worship the Lord with our systematic, proportionate giving.

PRAYER: Heavenly Father, teach us Thy ways. Teach us to walk in Thy ways. Help us to see that it is good to sow bountifully in every area of life. Give us eyes to see the reaping, in time and eternity. May our gifts today mean bountiful results in other lives, we pray in Jesus' name. Amen.

II CORINTHIANS 9:7

Every man according as he purposeth in his heart, so let him give; not grudgingly, or of necessity: for God loveth a cheerful giver.

In II Corinthians 9:7 we read, "Every man according as he purposeth in his heart, so let him give, not grudgingly, or of necessity; for God loveth a cheerful giver."

Our church agrees with God in this. As you prepare your offering, don't complain about giving; just give what you can give without complaining.

PRAYER: Heavenly Father, would we dare to complain about giving to Thee? If that is in our hearts, work in them to overcome it, till we give, not with a sense of responsibility only, but with a sense of privilege. Receive what we now cheerfully offer Thee through our Lord, Jesus Christ. Amen.

II CORINTHIANS 9:7

Every man according as he purposeth in his heart, so let him give; not grudgingly, or of necessity: for God loveth a cheerful giver.

Are you comfortable in your giving?

If you are giving more than you feel you can afford, giving more because you feel you ought to, the Lord is not pleased; for He says "not grudgingly, or of necessity; God loves the cheerful giver." Sacrificial giving is only for those who can be comfortable with it.

In this way let us worship the Lord with our systematic, proportionate giving.

PRAYER: Heavenly Father, giver of every good and perfect gift, we acknowledge Thee as our Lord and Provider, with our lips and with our substance, cheerfully given because it is given to Thee, through Jesus Christ, our Lord. Amen.

II CORINTHIANS 9:7

Every man according as he purposeth in his heart, so let him give; not grudgingly, or of necessity: for God loveth a cheerful giver.

"God loves a cheerful giver."

Why? Because cheerfulness indicates a grateful heart, one which recognizes that one has received more than he deserves. It indicates a compassionate heart, a heart like God's and a mind like Christ's. It indicates that grace has worked in our life to overcome selfishness and to teach us to trust God for all our needs.

May God see this about us as we worship Him with our tithes cheerfully offered.

PRAYER: *Heavenly Father, we are grateful. Make us compassionate, and overcome our selfishness that we may delight in helping spread the gospel and providing help for those in need. Note the attitude of our hearts as we give today, and correct them, if necessary. We pray in Jesus' name. Amen.*

II CORINTHIANS 9:7

Every man according as he purposeth in his heart, so let him give; not grudgingly, or of necessity: for God loveth a cheerful giver.

"Every man according as he purposeth in his heart, so let him give, not grudgingly, or of necessity, for God loveth a cheerful giver."

A sign in a restaurant reads, "Meals cash. We trusted a friend; he failed to pay. We lost the price of the meal, and the friend."

How true. When we withhold from a friend what belongs to him we eventually lose the enjoyment of his friendship. Is this not true as well with God? Would God not mean more to us if week by week we gave Him all that is His?

You see, we are not giving from our purse to the church, but from our heart to the Lord, as we worship Him with our cheerful, systematic and proportionate gifts.

PRAYER: *Heavenly Father, we know You could get along without us, without both our friendship and our substance, but You have desired both, and we would give You both today, giving You our time and our substance, which we offer now through Jesus, our Lord. Amen.*

Every man according as he purposeth in his heart, so let him give; not grudgingly, or of necessity: for God loveth a cheerful giver.

"Every man according as he purposeth in his heart, so let him give, not grudgingly, or of necessity; for God loveth a cheerful giver."

Those who attend church only occasionally are sometimes heard to say: "The church is always asking for money." But who is the church? It is not some abstract power out there with its hands out for money. It is the people who love the Lord saying, "We want to accomplish this or that for God, here or abroad, and we will give to accomplish it."

These are the ones who have the opportunity now to worship the Lord with their cheerful, purposeful gifts.

PRAYER: Thank You, Heavenly Father, for our material needs supplied. Thank You for Your saving grace so freely bestowed on us. And thank You for putting it into our hearts to give that others may know Your grace. Here are our gifts, offered willingly and cheerfully. Transform them into a spiritual power in human lives. In Jesus' name. Amen.

II CORINTHIANS 9:7

Every man according as he purposeth in his heart, so let him give; not grudgingly, or of necessity: for God loveth a cheerful giver.

"The Lord loves a cheerful giver." Who should give to support the Lord's work?

1. *Only* those who are the Lord's—III John 7: "They went forth, taking nothing of the heathen."

2. *All* who are the Lord's—I Corinthians 16:2: "Let every one of you lay by him in store as God has prospered him."

3. *All* whose needs have been supplied by the Lord—Matthew 10:8: "Freely ye have received; freely give."

4. *All* who want their needs supplied by the Lord—Philippians 4:19 is a promise written to those who have given for the Lord's work: "But my God shall supply all your need according to His riches in glory by Christ Jesus."

"*Every man*, according as he purposes in his heart, so let him give; not grudgingly, or of necessity; for God loveth a cheerful giver."

PRAYER: Heavenly Father, we acknowledge our debt to others who gave that we might hear the gospel and be taught Your Word. As your children, whose needs have been supplied, we present our offerings now, that others too might hear and grow in the grace of our Lord, Jesus Christ, in whose name we give. Amen.

II CORINTHIANS 9:8

And God is able to make all grace abound toward you; that ye, always having all sufficiency in all things, may abound to every good work.

Concerning giving, God makes it possible for us to do what we want to do for Him.

In II Corinthians 9:8, we read, "God is able to make all grace abound toward you, that ye, always having all sufficiency in all things, may abound to every good work."

What these Corinthian Christians had faith-promised a year before (see verse 2), God made it possible for them to give (see verse 8)—and He will do the same for us.

Let us count on His help as we worship the Lord with our good work of giving.

PRAYER: Heavenly Father, Your ways are marvelous, helping us to do what we want to do for You. We've set our goals; now by Your grace we bring our gifts and ask You to bless them as You have already blessed us. In Jesus' name. Amen.

II CORINTHIANS 9:10

Now he that ministereth seed to the sower both minister bread for your food, and multiply your seed sown, and increase the fruits of your righteousness.

"He that ministereth seed to the sower both minister bread for your food, and multiply your seed sown, and increase the fruits of your righteousness."

Because God wants us to have, He supplies our need. Because God wants us to share, He gives us more than we need. Then, whereas what we use for self is spent, what we use for others is invested and increases as fruit for God.

Let us worship the Lord as we invest what He has made possible.

PRAYER: Heavenly Father, thank You for seed and bread. We would invest some of the seed and share some of the bread in Your name. Multiply it in Your cause. We are grateful for the ability to give to the God we love. Amen.

Being enriched in every thing to all bountifulness, which causeth through us thanksgiving to God.

"We are enriched in everything to all bountifulness, causing through us thanksgiving to God."

God gives to us that we might give to others, and every time we pass on some of the substance God has given us, we cause those who receive it to give thanks to God; and so a full circle is made, from God to us, to others, to God.

Let us give from what we have been given and complete that circle as we worship the Lord with our systematic, proportionate giving.

PRAYER: Heavenly Father, thank You for all we receive. Help us to realize that what you give us is not all to remain with us, but that some is to be passed on to others who have less. May needy ones have a reason to give thanks, as we give help today through our Lord, Jesus Christ. Amen.

II CORINTHIANS 9:12

For the administration of this service not only supplieth the want of the saints, but is abundant also by many thanksgivings unto God.

How many people around the world, do you suppose, have heard the gospel and been saved because you gave of your substance to meet their need? Every time they thank God for their salvation, it is thanks given for your gift.

Second Corinthians 9:12 says, "The delivering of your gifts not only supplies a need, but results in a wealth of thanksgivings to God—a sea of upturned faces giving thanks to God."

It is not that man or God will praise *us*, but people will praise *Him* for *our* gifts.

Let us sow for a rich harvest of thanksgiving to God, as we worship the Lord with our systematic, proportionate giving.

PRAYER: Heavenly Father, may we be as impressed with spiritual values, which are eternal, as we are with the things of the world that will pass away. Inspire us to invest a proper portion in the salvation of our fellow-men. As we deliver our gifts today we pray that they may be used to save many. In Jesus' name. Amen.

II CORINTHIANS 9:13

Whiles by the experiment of this ministration they glorify God for your professed subjection unto the gospel of Christ, and for your liberal distribution unto them, and unto all men.

Those who benefit by our giving "glorify God for our subjection unto the gospel of Christ," which is the upreach of faith—the Godward side; "and for our generous-hearted liberality," which is the outreach of faith—the manward side. God is honored by our faith which we profess, and by our giving which proves our profession.

Let us demonstrate our faith today as we worship the Lord with our generous-hearted liberality.

PRAYER: Heavenly Father, in the spirit of our Savior who came not to be ministered unto, but to minister and to give His life a ransom for many, may we give today, through Jesus Christ, our Lord. Amen.

II CORINTHIANS 9:15
(Christmas)

Thanks be unto God for his unspeakable gift.

"Thanks be unto God for his unspeakable gift."

Christ was the first Christmas gift, given by God to the world. Christ is still the best gift we can give for Christmas.

Numberless multitudes in this world have never even heard of this gift; they have not had the opportunity to receive it. We can give Christ to them by:

1. Witnessing to those around us.
2. Going to those far away.
3. Giving gifts to help get the gospel out to them.

This is the purpose of our offerings. Through this church we give to Christ in order to *give* Christ. Let us worship the Christ of Christmas with our tithes and offerings.

PRAYER: Heavenly Father, thank You for Your wonderful Gift, undeserved, unsolicited, and often unappreciated. Put Your love in our hearts for the undeserving, and may none be denied the gift of eternal life because we have failed to give in proper measure. Here are our gifts of love this Christmas, offered through Your Gift, Jesus, our Lord. Amen.

II CORINTHIANS 9:15

Thanks be unto God for his unspeakable gift.

After two chapters about the how and why of Christian giving, II Corinthians 8 and 9, Paul sums up all the motivation, reason, incentive, and measure in one sentence, II Corinthians 9:15, "Thanks be unto God for His unspeakable gift."

It is in response to this unsparing, immeasurable gift of Christ, from which we have benefited so much, that all our giving flows, as we worship the Lord with our systematic, proportionate gifts.

PRAYER: Heavenly Father, we thank You for Your Gift, which is great beyond description, and for what He has done in our lives. To Him and to You we give today, gifts that are measured by our loving gratitude for Jesus Christ, our Lord. Amen.

II CORINTHIANS 8 and 9

A Mrs. B. N. Brown must have been thinking of II Corinthians 8 and 9, for she summed up the two chapters well when she wrote:

Give: Not because you must, but because you may;
Not out of your abundance, but out of your very living;
Not from a sense of duty, but rather of a recognition of your high privilege;
Not in a spirit of self-righteousness, but in a spirit of profound righteousness;
So may the blessing of God be yours in fullness.

May we give in this spirit as we worship the Lord with our tithes and offerings.

PRAYER: Heavenly Father, we have things yet to learn about giving, but we would give with these attitudes. Indeed, it is in this way we bring our gifts today and offer them in the merit of our Savior, Jesus. Amen.

Wherefore then serveth the law? It was added because of transgressions, till the seed should come to whom the promise was made; and it was ordained by angels in the hand of a mediator.

Like all the items of the Law, tithing was added because of transgression, until Christ should come. It had been a principle of stewardship from the beginning. Thus, the fulfilling of the Law, in Christ, puts us back on the principle basis, rather than under Law.

Christians do not tithe because they have to, or neglect it because they don't have to; but practice it because they recognize it as good—a good principle, a good stewardship, an act that honors God.

We are not under the Law, but under grace; therefore let us worship the Lord with our tithes and offerings.

PRAYER: Heavenly Father, help us to rise above our self-interest sufficiently to see the value of giving, the good of sharing, the inherent good in the principles of stewardship You have laid down, and then help us to follow them faithfully. Here are our gifts today. Examine them to see that we are fulfilling the righteousness of the Law, as we offer them in Jesus' name. Amen.

GALATIANS 5:6

For in Jesus Christ neither circumcision availeth any thing, nor uncircumcision; but faith which worketh by love.

The Christian's rule for giving is the same as his rule for all things—"faith which works by love" (Galatians 5:6). Love prompts us to give. Faith trusts God to provide.

The best way to show our love in giving is by systematic, proportionate giving. A wife appreciates hubby's candy and flowers on special occasions, but what really counts is his faithful care of her day by day, and letting her share in all he has. True love to God will express itself the same way.

With faith working by love, let us worship the Lord with our systematic, proportionate giving.

PRAYER: Heavenly Father, we would express both our faith and our love by the measure of our giving today; not giving less than we ought; not giving grudgingly or of necessity; but giving liberally out of love for our Lord, Jesus Christ, in whose name we present our offerings. Amen.

Be not deceived; God is not mocked: for whatsoever a man soweth, that shall he also reap.

Concerning sharing, or giving, God says, "Whatsoever a man sows, that shall he also reap" (Galatians 6:7).

In a paraphrase of that, Charles Shedd taught his children, "What goes from your pocket has a direct bearing on what comes in."

This is true in several ways. What you give affects your prosperity according to God's laws. What you save affects your security and peace. And what you spend buys things that affect your body, mind, soul, and spirit.

It has been found that giving 10 percent, saving 10 percent, and spending the rest thankfully—in that order—is the economic key to a good life.

Let us have in mind what we would like to reap as we sow our tithes and offerings this morning.

PRAYER: Heavenly Father, how gracious of You to add to our blessings when we share with others. Help us to learn your economic laws, and to trust you for these as much as we trust you for salvation. Cause our gifts today to do good to others, we pray in Jesus' name. Amen.

EPHESIANS 4:28

Let him that stole steal no more: but rather let him labour, working with his hands the thing which is good, that he may have to give to him that needeth.

Stealing is the opposite of sharing. Those who steal take what belongs to others for themselves; those who share give what belongs to themselves for others. The Christian ethic is "Let him that stole steal no more but, rather, let him labor . . . that he may have to give to him that needeth."

As Christians, we would not simply stop stealing and keep what we have; we go all the way and start giving. We can do it this morning as we worship the Lord with our gifts for those in need.

PRAYER: Heavenly Father, thank You for the grace that not only saves, but changes us. Change us with regard to our natural selfishness. Give us the mind of Christ, a mind for others. Teach us to share. Guide us in our sharing. And use our sharing to enrich others, we ask in Jesus' name. Amen.

Look not every man on his own things, but every man also on the things of others.

Jesus commended the widow who gave two mites, not because of how much she gave, but because of the percentage she gave—she gave her all.

What we can afford to give is based not on what we have left after spending for ourselves, but on what we are willing to do without, and this is what brings His commendation. "Look not every man on his own things, but every man also on the things of others" (Philippians 2:4).

Let us be sure that we have His commendation as we worship the Lord with our systematic, proportionate giving.

PRAYER: Heavenly Father, help us to love our neighbor as ourselves, and to give so they may have what they need for soul and body. Deliver us from selfishness. Give us a generous spirit. Use our gifts today to help others, we pray in Jesus' name. Amen.

PHILIPPIANS 2:4

Look not every man on his own things, but every man also on the the things of others.

"Look not every man on his own things, but every man also on the things of others."

Our giving is determined by one of two things: greed or need; self or others.

Consider the widow with the cruse of oil. Greed would have said, "I can't spare it" and as a result she would have run out. Need said, "I will give it" and she was taken care of.

Consider also the widow with the mite. Greed would have said, "I can't afford it." But motivated by need, she gave her all, and she was commended.

We say we can't afford to give more. That could be selfish greed. If we would do without some of the things which are not real needs, we would have more to give for the needs of others.

"Seek not every man his own wealth, but anothers' " (I Corinthians 10:24).

Let us be motivated by the needs of others as we worship the Lord with our systematic, proportionate gifts.

PRAYER: Heavenly Father, it was because of our need that You spared not Your own son, but delivered Him up for us all. May such love be in our hearts, to direct our giving. In Jesus' name. Amen.

Look not every man on his own things, but every man also on the things of others.

WORLD CALL

I planned an ultra modern home, but a Korean citizen whispered, "I have no home at all!"

I dreamed of a country place for the pleasure of my children, but an exiled lad kept saying, "I have no country!"

I decided on a new cupboard right now, but a child of Africa cried out, "I have no cup!"

I started to purchase a new kind of washing machine, but an Indian woman said softly, "I have nothing to wash!"

I wanted a quick-freezing unit for storing quantities of food, but across the waters came the cry, "I have no food!"

I ordered a new car for the pleasure of my loved ones, but an Arab orphan sobbed, "I have no loved ones!"

I planned a stained-glass window above the choir stalls, but a Mexican pastor murmured softly, "My church has no walls!"

Author Unknown

"Do not merely consider your own desires, but also the needs of others," as we worship the Lord with our tithes and offerings.

PRAYER: *Heavenly Father, of wanting things there is no end, and of needs there is no end. We pray, make us willing to limit the indulgence of our wants by loving our neighbor as ourselves, and giving to meet his need. May others have occasion to give thanks for our offerings today, we pray in Jesus' name. Amen.*

PHILIPPIANS 2:5

Let this mind be in you, which was also in Christ Jesus.

The economic demands of life are a constant threat to giving, unless we practice systematic, proportionate giving. We will never have enough to give unless we budget our giving.

True Christianity recognizes a balance between meeting the needs of self and meeting the needs of others, of loving thy neighbor as thyself. And the committed Christian will not permit himself to upset that balance; rather, he will deny himself in order to help others in their deepest need.

"Let this mind be in you, which was also in Christ Jesus"—a mind concerned with the needs of others—as we worship the Lord with our tithes and offerings.

PRAYER: Heavenly Father, may the mind of Christ our Savior live in us from day to day; His love and unselfishness controlling all we do and say—and give. May we ever adequately share what we have with others who have less, especially those who do not have the gospel of our Lord, Jesus Christ, through whom we offer these gifts. Amen.

PHILIPPIANS 2:21

For all seek their own, not the things which are Jesus Christ's.

"All seek their own, not the things which are Jesus Christ's." Paul might well have written that about so-called Christian America. In our nation, for every dollar given by Protestants, Catholics, and Jews, 750 dollars are spent for pleasure.

This may not be true of many worshiping with us today, but it alerts us to the importance of systematic, proportionate giving, so that we give God a proper percentage of our income; so let us examine our sense of values, and see that we are laying up treasure where moth and rust do not corrupt, and where thieves do not break through and steal.

Let us seek the things which are Christ's as we worship the Lord with our tithes and offerings.

PRAYER: Heavenly Father, forgive us for constantly seeking things for earthly pleasure, when we might be seeking the things of Christ and of lasting value. Put a desire in our hearts to give unto One who has given so much to us. Just as we love You because You first loved us, so may we give to You because You first gave to us. May our gifts this morning be acceptable in Your sight, as we offer them in the merit of Your son, Jesus. Amen.

Notwithstanding ye have well done, that ye did communicate with my affliction.

Paul wrote to his friends in Philippi, "You have done well in sharing with my affliction." This is what giving is all about—sharing with others who have less, materially or spiritually; and no matter how little we have, there is always someone in the world who has less.

We speak of worshiping God with our tithes and offerings, but it is impossible to give to God without giving to man, recognizing his need and being concerned about it. This is well, indeed.

Let us do well as we worship the Lord by sharing our tithes and offerings.

PRAYER: Heavenly Father, may our worship be more than empty words. May our giving be an act of true worship, as it reflects Your concern for the afflicted. Teach us so to share and do well in Your sight. In Jesus' name. Amen.

PHILIPPIANS 4:14
(Missionary)

Notwithstanding ye have well done, that ye did communicate with my affliction.

Paul, the missionary, wrote to his friends in Phillipi (4:14), "You have done well in sharing with my affliction," referring to the offerings they sent him.

If each of our missionaries could send a telegram this morning, they would probably say the same thing. Part of all we give goes to the Lord's servants, whose affliction is the burden of their work. We do well, indeed, when we help to lighten their burden by our giving.

Let us share with them now as we worship the Lord with our systematic, proportionate gifts.

PRAYER: Heavenly Father, we are grateful to those who have gone into the harvest fields of the world in obedience to Your call, and we are glad to have a part in their ministry. May we relieve them of unnecessary burdens by adequate financial support. May our offerings take into consideration their needs, as we present them through Jesus Christ, our Lord. Amen.

PHILIPPIANS 4:15
(Missionary)

Now ye Philippians know also, that in the beginning of the gospel, when I departed from Macedonia, no church communicated with me as concerning giving and receiving, but ye only.

Paul, in his missionary efforts, had established several churches. But when he left Macedonia to continue his missionary work and reach others, he wrote to the Philippians that they were the only church that shared with him a part of their offerings (Philippians 4:15).

It is true now, as then, that many churches are willing to receive the gospel, but then are too concerned with building their own work, and don't adequately share a vision and concern for those without the gospel.

"Freely ye have received; freely give." God will bless the church that has a missionary vision and concern.

Part of our sharing is for missions, as we worship the Lord with our systematic, proportionate giving.

PRAYER: Heavenly Father, we are grateful for all whose giving made it possible for us to hear the gospel and be helped in a church. Now we want others to have that privilege, and to that end we present our offerings to Thee today, through Jesus Christ, our Lord. Amen.

PHILIPPIANS 4:16
(Missionary)

For even in Thessalonica ye sent once and again unto my necessity.

Paul, the missionary, commended the Christians in Philippi because, he said, "ye sent once and again unto my necessity"—you sent more than once to relieve my need. These fine Christians, recognizing that they themselves had daily, recurring needs, realized the same might be true of the servants of Christ far away. And they gave, not once—to quiet their conscience—but time and again—to express their love and concern.

Those with the love of Christ in their hearts never get tired of giving. As long as their needs are supplied, they share with others.

Let us thoughtfully share as we worship the Lord with our systematic, proportionate giving.

PRAYER: Heavenly Father, may we realize that these underpaid servants of yours do have needs. Put in our hearts the zeal to help them often. Today we give to relieve their necessity, through Jesus Christ, our Lord. Amen.

Not because I desire a gift: but I desire fruit that may abound to your account.

Concerning giving by the people he had preached to, Paul said, "Not because I desire a gift; but I desire fruit that may abound to your account." "I want you to give, not for my sake, but for your sake."

May the Lord help us pastors to always be free of ulterior motives when we speak about giving.

Paul's word is in harmony with all Scripture, which teaches that giving does more for the giver than for the ones who receive.

May our giving today be regarded by God as fruit for our account, as we worship Him with our systematic, proportionate gifts.

PRAYER: Heavenly Father, we would lay up treasure in heaven; we would have reason to be glad when we stand before the judgment seat of Christ; we would have eternal fruit from our temporal possessions. And so we bring these tithes and offerings to Thee this morning, through our Lord, Jesus Christ. Amen.

PHILIPPIANS 4:17

Not because I desire a gift: but I desire fruit that may abound to your account.

Concerning the giving of Christians, Philippians 4:17 says, "It is fruit that will abound to your account," or "It is a harvest of blessing that is accumulating to your account."

Our giving is more than a present deduction from our income tax. It is an investment in the future, which will bring rich dividends from the Lord to whom we give. If we invest liberally, we will reap liberally.

This should help us decide what we will give, as we worship the Lord with our systematic, proportionate giving.

PRAYER: Heavenly Father, thank You for those who invested in us and our salvation. Now we would invest in the salvation and spiritual growth of others, by giving to You through the church. May our church use it wisely for a maximum harvest of blessing, we pray in Jesus' name. Amen.

But I have all, and abound, I am full, having received of Epaphroditus the things which were sent from you, an odour of a sweet smell, a sacrifice acceptable, well-pleasing to God.

Philippians 4:18 speaks of giving which supplies the needs of others as "the sweet fragrance of a sacrifice which is acceptable and well-pleasing to God": "your generosity is like a lovely fragrance; a sacrifice that pleases the very heart of God."

Of course, it can only do this when it is unselfish giving, giving that regards the needs of others as well as self.

May our giving this morning be such a sweet incense, as we worship the Lord with our tithes and offerings.

PRAYER: Heavenly Father, teach us so to give that our offerings will be generous, fragrant sacrifices that please Thee. There is nothing we would rather do than please Thee, in this, as in all other ways. Receive our sacrifice, and use it for the work of Christ, in whose merit we present it. Amen.

PHILIPPIANS 4:19

But my God shall supply all your need according to his riches in glory by Christ Jesus.

To those who share with others in their need, the Bible promises, "but my God shall supply all your need according to His riches in glory by Christ Jesus."

One of our members gives this testimony: "I can testify to no 'spectacular' result of making a faith-promise; but I have been making these promises throughout my life and have never gone without necessities. God provides strength for additional work to earn the additional amount. Life is surely interesting as I watch Him provide." You can have the joy of such an experience, too.

From what He has provided, let us worship the Lord with our systematic, proportionate giving.

PRAYER: Heavenly Father, as Your children, we testify of Your faithfulness and goodness. It has been a joy to watch You provide. May our love and faith be strengthened, that we may dare to give that the gospel may be preached to every creature. Use our offerings today to that end, we pray in Jesus' name. Amen.

PHILIPPIANS 4:19

But my God shall supply all your need according to his riches in glory by Christ Jesus.

A Scotch woman with several children was left a widow. She had little money and had a hard time getting along. But she trusted God and told her children to do so.

One day, however, she ran out of money entirely and was down to the last cup of flour, with no idea where any more would come from. As she was scraping the flour out to make a meal, her faith wavered and tears came to her eyes. Her little boy noticed it and said, "Why are you crying mother? Doesn't God hear you scrape the bottom of the barrel?"

God does know our need, and has promised that when we give to meet the needs of others, He will meet our need. It was to a church of giving people that Philippians 4:19 was written—"But my God shall supply all your need according to his riches in glory by Christ Jesus."

Let us assure our own prosperity as we worship the Lord with our systematic, proportionate giving.

PRAYER: Heavenly Father, thank You for the faith of little children. May our faith be as simple and complete, and may our compassion for others be like Yours. In trust and concern we give this morning, through Jesus Christ, our Lord. Amen.

PHILIPPIANS 4:19

But my God shall supply all your need according to his riches in glory by Christ Jesus.

Every time we gather for worship, there are over one million more mouths to feed than there were the week before; and over one million more people to reach with the gospel. But we can, with gladness, give for the never-ending task from His never-ending supply. For to those who share, the Bible says, "But my God shall supply all your need according to His riches in glory by Christ Jesus." From His supply, let us worship the Lord with our systematic, proportionate giving.

PRAYER: Heavenly Father, we may not see all these new people, but give us an awareness of them, nevertheless, that we may be moved to do our part to give them the words of eternal life, through Jesus Christ, our Lord. Amen.

PHILIPPIANS 4:19
(Missionary)

But my God shall supply all your need according to his riches in glory by Christ Jesus.

"My God shall supply all your need according to His riches in glory by Christ Jesus." The church that shares with its missionaries (verse 14) is assured of having its own needs provided, contrary to human wisdom.

In fact, every promise of God to supply our needs is contingent on our supplying the needs of someone else with less than we. Only by giving can we be in the line of blessing.

We benefit others and ourselves as we worship the Lord with our systematic, proportionate giving.

PRAYER: Heavenly Father, we thank Thee for all we have here in our church facilities and ministry, and for those who have gone forth to carry the gospel to the uttermost parts of the earth. We want them to be adequately supported in their important ministry, and so we give for the work, both at home and abroad, through Jesus Christ, our Lord. Amen.

I TIMOTHY 5:17-18
(For Special Speakers)

Let the elders that rule well be counted worthy of double honour, especially they who labour in the word and doctrine. For the scripture saith, Thou shalt not muzzle the ox that treadeth out the corn. And, The labourer is worthy of his reward.

Let those be counted worthy of double honor who labor in the Word . . . for the Scripture says the laborer is worthy of his reward.

Our offering today is a love offering for _____, who has sown unto us spiritual things for the soul, and is entitled to reap our things for the body (I Corinthians 9:11).

Let us take abundant care of this worthy servant of the Lord as we worship God with our proportionate gifts.

PRAYER: Heavenly Father, thank You for those who liberally minister the Bread of life to our souls. We would liberally minister to the physical necessities of life for them, and thus bring our offerings today, through Jesus Christ, our Lord. May their need be met. Amen.

I TIMOTHY 5:17-18
(Missionary)

Let the elders that rule well be counted worthy of double honour, especially they who labour in the word and doctrine. For the scripture saith, Thou shalt not muzzle the ox that treadeth out the corn. And, The labourer is worthy of his reward.

Side by side, in I Timothy 5:16-18, are instructions that we are to support our own families and also the families of our missionaries and others who minister the Word of God. God recognizes our responsibility for our families, but does not accept that as an excuse for neglecting the families of His servants.

It is to this end that we worship the Lord with our systematic, proportionate giving.

PRAYER: Heavenly Father, as we rejoice in the abundant supply of all of our needs, may we be concerned that your servants be adequately supported, and give in such a measure that they can be. If they have special needs today, supply them according to your riches in glory, by Christ Jesus, in whose name we make our offering now. Amen.

I TIMOTHY 6:6

But godliness with contentment is great gain.

"Godliness with contentment is great gain." Getting ahead is not getting more material goods, but more spiritual grace, and being content with what we have of a material nature. This is not the wisdom of the world, but of those taught by the Spirit.

Such understanding helps us, as we worship the Lord with our systematic, proportionate giving.

PRAYER: Heavenly Father, teach us to be content with the things we have and to avoid covetousness. We press on to lay hold of Your high calling to be like Christ Jesus, by whose merit we present our tithes and offerings now. Amen.

For we brought nothing into this world, and it is certain we can carry nothing out.

"We brought nothing into this world, and it is certain we can carry nothing out." But we *can* send it on *ahead*! Whatever we spend on ourselves is gone. What we give for others lasts forever. What we save for ourselves we must give up in the end. What we give for others will be waiting for us at the end.

"Lay not up for your *self* treasure upon earth, where moth and rust doth corrupt and where thieves break through and steal, but lay up for your *self* treasure in heaven."

This is what we do each time we worship the Lord with our systematic, proportionate giving.

PRAYER: Heavenly Father, help us to understand the true meaning of our possessions, what they can do for us and others in time and in eternity. May we not be attached to them overmuch. Open our hands from their natural clenched position, and make them hands that dispense help to others. Receive our tithes and offerings today through Jesus Christ, our Lord. Amen.

I TIMOTHY 6:10

For the love of money is the root of all evil: which while some coveted after, they have erred from the faith and pierced themselves through with many sorrows.

"The love of money is a root of all kinds of evil."

Some Christians do not practice proportionate giving because they love money—love to know they have some. They have money in the bank they are not using now, but they want to put more there because they love to have it, and so they do not give. Their love of money results in the evil of not practicing systematic, proportionate giving as God supplies their need week by week.

Let us deny this love, as we express our love for the Lord with our tithes and offerings.

PRAYER: Heavenly Father, deliver us from the love of money. Make us good stewards of it in spending, saving, and giving, but deliver us from coveting it. And may we see our possessions, not simply as something to have, but something to share, liberally and cheerfully, as we do now through our Lord, Jesus Christ. Amen.

I TIMOTHY 6:10

For the love of money is the root of all evil: which while some coveted after, they have erred from the faith, and pierced themselves through with many sorrows.

"The love of money is a root of many evils," including the evils of selfishness, indifference to the needs of others, withholding for self more than is proper, failing to honor God with the first fruits of all our increase, and failing to lay up treasure in heaven. Regular, proportionate giving is a good cure for this.

Let us honor God and think of others, as we worship the Lord with our tithes and offerings.

PRAYER: Heavenly Father, the love of money has caused all of us to commit some of these evils. We would learn to value money, not for the excess things it can do for us, but as an instrument in our hands with which to meet the lack of others. To that end we give today, with the prayer it may give others cause for thanksgiving. In Jesus' name. Amen.

I TIMOTHY 6:17-19

Charge them that are rich in this world, that they be not highminded, nor trust in uncertain riches, but in the living God, who giveth us richly all things to enjoy; that they do good, that they be rich in good works, ready to distribute, willing to communicate; laying up in store for themselves a good foundation against the time to come, that they may lay hold on eternal life.

"Charge them that are rich in this world, that they be not high-minded, nor trust in uncertain riches, but in the living God, who giveth us richly all things to enjoy; that they do good, that they be rich in good works, ready to distribute, willing to communicate; laying up in store for themselves a good foundation against the time to come, that they may lay hold on eternal life."

If we have the means to enjoy the material things of this world, we are to share with others in need. Then, instead of all being spent, what we give is invested for eternal reward

Let us have this in mind as we worship the Lord with our systematic, proportionate gifts.

PRAYER: Heavenly Father, let us not apply this Scripture passage to those who have more than we, but help us to see ourselves as those who have more than others. Make us willing to share, becoming rich in good works. May others be blessed by our distribution. In Jesus' name. Amen.

Charge them that are rich in this world, that they be not highminded, nor trust in uncertain riches, but in the living God, who giveth us richly all things to enjoy; that they do good, that they be rich in good works, ready to distribute, willing to communicate; laying up in store for themselves a good foundation against the time to come, that they may lay hold on eternal life.

According to the Word of God in I Timothy 6:17-19, to be rich in good works is better than to be rich in material substance (for good works both abide and satisfy); to share is better than to keep; to trust God is better than to trust in uncertain riches.

With these thoughts as our guide, let us worship the Lord with our proportionate gifts.

PRAYER: Heavenly Father, Your wisdom is so contrary to our natural inclination, and yet so right. May Your wisdom overcome our inclination, that we may give as we ought. May others be enriched by our giving today through Jesus Christ, our Lord. Amen.

I TIMOTHY 6:18-19

That they do good, that they be rich in good works, ready to distribute, willing to communicate; laying up in store for themselves a good foundation against the time to come, that they may lay hold on eternal life.

"Wouldn't you really rather have a . . . "

This is the slogan of our times. "Having" is the world's idea of really living. But the Bible teaches that really living is not having, but giving!

First Timothy 6:18-19 reads, "Be ready to share . . . be generous in giving . . . treasuring up for yourself what, in the future, will prove to be a good foundation, and so laying hold on what is really life."

It is this we are laying hold of, when we worship the Lord with our systematic, proportionate giving.

PRAYER: Heavenly Father, we build our little, personal economic kingdoms, knowing all the while that they will crumble in time and be left behind. Teach us each week to lay blocks that will prove to be a good foundation for an eternal kingdom. Direct the use of our sharing money, offered to Thee today in the merit of Christ, our Savior and Lord. Amen.

II TIMOTHY 2:10

Therefore I endure all things for the elect's sake, that they may also obtain the salvation which is in Christ Jesus with eternal glory.

Paul said, "I endure all things for the elect's sake, that they may also obtain the salvation which is in Christ Jesus."

His point was that although Christ paid for our salvation, we must also pay if others are to be saved. Faith comes by hearing, but how shall they hear except some be sent? "Unto us it is given, on behalf of Christ, not only to believe on him, but also to suffer for his sake." Is our giving really costing us anything? Has it been a sacrifice? David said, "I will not give to the Lord that which cost me nothing."

Let us weigh our giving in this light as we worship the Lord with our proportionate gifts.

PRAYER: Heavenly Father, help us to really share Your concern for men and women without salvation, and to so give that they will be able to hear. Use our gifts today for this purpose, here and abroad, we pray in Jesus' name. Amen.

HEBREWS 13:15-16
(Thanksgiving)

By him therefore let us offer the sacrifice of praise to God continually, that is, the fruit of our lips giving thanks to his name. But to do good and to communicate forget not: for with such sacrifices God is well pleased.

Thanksgiving would not be complete without an opportunity to do something for others. Those who are truly grateful seek opportunity to thankfully give.

"By him let us continually offer up a sacrifice of praise to God, that is, the fruit of our lips giving thanks to his name; but to do good and to share, forget not, for with such sacrifices God is well pleased."

Let us worship the Lord with a sacrifice of sharing at this Thanksgiving time.

PRAYER: Our prayer is in the words of Janie Alford (source unknown):
I do not thank Thee, Lord, that I have bread to eat while others starve;
Nor yet for work to do while empty hands solicit heaven;
Nor for a body strong while other bodies flatten beds of pain;
No, not for these do I give thanks!
But I am grateful, Lord, because my meager loaf I may divide;
And that my busy hands may move to meet another's need;
Because my doubled strength I may expend to steady one who faints.
Yea, for all these do I give thanks. Amen.

128

I PETER 4:10

As every man hath received the gift, even so minister the same one to another, as good stewards of the manifold grace of God.

William L. Stidger, in *Human Adventures in Happy Living*, says,

One of the most fascinating observations I have made in interviewing great creative personalities is that they all seem to have the spirit of Christian service in their souls. There is, for instance, Fritz Kreisler, the world's most famous violinist. Kreisler says that none of the money he earns through his music is his, but is a gift of God, and he is only the steward of that music and that money. One day in Berlin, Germany, when I was lunching in his very humble home, he said to me, "I have never owned a home, because a home would stand between me and all the homeless of the world. I have never eaten luxurious meals, if I could help it, because that meal would stand between me and the hungry of the world.

This is the attitude commended in I Peter 4:10, "As each one has received . . . use it in serving one another, as good stewards of the manifold grace of God."

With such a sense of stewardship, let us worship the Lord with our proportionate giving.

PRAYER: Heavenly Father, we thank Thee for the inspiration of men who have learned to think of others as well as themselves; and especially our Lord Jesus, who, though He was rich, yet for our sakes became poor, that we through His poverty might be rich. In His name we present our offerings now. Amen.

I JOHN 3:17

But whoso hath this world's good, and seeth his brother have need, and shutteth up his bowels of compassion from him, how dwelleth the love of God in him?

"Any one who has this world's good, and seeth his brother have need, and closes his heart of compassion from him, how is it possible the love of God dwells in him?"

In other words, what we give to help people, for body or soul, reflects our love of God, whether we want it to, or not.

"Let us not love in word, or in tongue; but in deed and in truth" (verse 18) as we worship the Lord with our systematic, proportionate giving.

PRAYER: Heavenly Father, may Thy love for those in need be shed abroad in our hearts by the Holy Spirit given to us; and may it not be stifled by any selfishness on our part. We dedicate our gifts to Thee today, to alleviate the spiritual and temporal needs of our fellowman, through Jesus Christ, our Lord. Amen.

III JOHN 7
(Missionary)

Because that for his name's sake they went forth, taking nothing of the Gentiles.

Concerning support of the early missionaries, we read in verse 7 of the Third Epistle of John, "For His name's sake they went forth, taking nothing of the unsaved."

Our missionaries do the same, and part of our giving is for their support. John says we should help them after a godly sort, that is, adequately, equally, ungrudgingly; and in so doing we become fellow-helpers to the truth, and do well.

Let us do well as we worship the Lord with our systematic, proportionate giving, after a godly sort.

PRAYER: Heavenly Father, thank You for those committed Christians who dare go out in faith, looking not to the world, but to You for support. May we be willing instruments of that support, and so give that there may be equality. If today's gifts are not adequate, teach us. We want to please You in all things. Thank You for Your Unspeakable Gift, by whom we offer our gifts. Amen.